DISCIPLINE

TRAINING THE **MIND** TO MANAGE YOUR LIFE

HARRIS KERN | KAREN WILLI

Author of *Discipline: Six Steps to Unleashing Your Hidden Potential*

ISBN: 1-4033-6723-X (e-book)
ISBN: 1-4033-6724-8 (Paperback)
ISBN: 1-4033-6725-6 (Dustjacket)

This book is printed on acid free paper.

1stBooks – rev. 12/05/02

Table of Contents

FOREWORD VII

PREFACE XIII

DOING MORE WITH LESS XIII
PEOPLE ARE NOT EXCELLING XIV

DEDICATION XIX

ACKNOWLEDGEMENTS XXI

1. INTRODUCTION.. 1

LIFE IS ALL ABOUT ACCOMPLISHMENTS 1
A WORLD OF HURT 3
YOU HAVE THE POWER 7
AGE HAS NOTHING TO DO WITH IT 8
STATUS QUO IS FAILURE 9
DON'T WAIT UNTIL TOMORROW 10

2. PERSONALLY REGULATED IMPROVEMENT MODEL TO
EXCEL 12

IT'S NOT A TEAM EVENT 18
THE HIGH COST OF DEPENDENCE 19
A BLESSING OR A CURSE? 20
YOUR CURRENT ROUTINE 21
RECOMMENDED ROUTINE 29
STRUCTURE.. 36
MY CURRENT ROUTINE 37
MAKE YOUR ROUTINE PUBLIC KNOWLEDGE.............................. 38
SUGGESTIONS FOR MAKING THE LEAP TO THE PRIME OF YOUR LIFE 38
CREATIVE TIME SAVERS 39
MY PRIME ROUTINE 44

TOOLS OF THE TRADE 45
CHOOSE YOUR WEAPON 46
THE GIFT OF TIME 46

3.   YOUR LIFE, INC. 48

NEVER COMPARE YOURSELF TO SOMEONE ELSE 51
FEEL GOOD ABOUT YOURSELF 51
OBSTACLES 52
TEMPTATIONS 52
WORKING HARD 54
CONTINUOUSLY CHALLENGE YOURSELF 55
COMMITMENT 55
HAVING FUN 56
BEING UNCONVENTIONAL 57
NEVER BE SATISFIED 58
THERE'S ALWAYS A SOLUTION 59
DIGNITY 60
THE BUF FACTOR 61
BALANCE 61
SENSE OF URGENCY 62
FOCUS 63
KEEPING YOUR COOL 65
HOPE 65
THE NEGATIVE SIDE AFFECT 66

4.   TIME 69

EQUATE TIME TO MONEY 69
DON'T SIT AROUND WASTING TIME 72
TREAT ALL DAYS EQUALLY 75
STANDING IN LINE 78
IF ALL ELSE FAILS, WORK THAT LINE! 79
THE WORLD ON TIME 80

5.   SLEEP 82

MINIMIZING SLEEP 82
TECHNIQUES 83

EXCESSIVE SLEEP 84
WHEN WE CAN'T SLEEP 84
KILLER SLEEP STUDY 85
MAKE IT A GOAL 86
WE'RE NOT ALONE 87

6.   TRAINING THE MIND 89

PLAYING MIND GAMES 90
PSYCHING YOURSELF OUT IS CHILD'S PLAY 91
MOST FREQUENTLY USED EXCUSES 92
SOLUTIONS FOR THOSE EXCUSES 92
BEING REDUNDANT 109
MIND OVER MATTER 109
BEAUTIFUL MINDS 109
TRAINED MINDS WE ADMIRE 110
REFINED MINDS 110
ENORMOUS MENTAL FORTITUDE 111

7.   THE TOTAL PACKAGE 112

THE BODY TOO 112
STAY AHEAD OF THE GAME 113
PUSH YOUR BODY - IT CAN TAKE IT 113
MAKE EXERCISE FUN 114
EATING SMART 117
WHAT TO EAT AND WHEN 118
VALUES 120
LEARN FROM OTHERS 122
ONLY THE STRONG WILL SURVIVE 123

8.   IT'S NEVER ENOUGH 124

THE CONTINUOUS THIRST FOR KNOWLEDGE 124
PATIENCE 125
IT'S MUCH MORE THAN BEING A LEADER 125
MASTERS OF MENTAL STIMULATION 127
DISCIPLINED 130
BENEFITS 130

SUMMARY 138
IT'S NOT ABOUT MONEY 139
FAILURE WILL NOT BE IN YOUR VOCABULARY 140

9.   RETIREMENT 141

PLAN YOUR FUTURE, OR OTHERS WILL GLADLY PLAN IT FOR YOU 142
REDIRECTING MYSELF TOWARDS IMPASSIONED RECREATIONAL
EXPLOITS DAILY 143
BACK TO THE FUTURE 143
PUBLICIZE YOUR ROUTINE 144
UNPRIMED SENIORS 144

10.   EPILOG..146

IN LIFE AND IN DEATH 146
THE LEGACY 147
DO IT FOR THE CHILDREN..148
SPEND TIME ON YOUR KIDS, NOT MONEY.......................................149
ELDERSHIP...153

HK'S ANECDOTES 157

HK'S MOST COMMON PHRASES OF THE UNPRIMED: 157
HK'S FAVORITE REMARKS: 162
HK'S TIME WASTELAND: 165
HK'S QUOTES: 167
HK'S GRIEVANCES...170

BIBLIOGRAPHY 173

FOREWORD

This book is about your life and how to make the best of every minute of it from now on. It will teach you how to train your mind to manage your life. The one thing that is lacking in our society is the most critical tool that we all need to consistently strive to be better. In one word, it's Discipline. If you are looking for a quick fix to make yourself a better person, we are here to tell you that no such thing exists. You have to be willing to work for this because nothing worthwhile comes easy. And there is nothing more worthwhile to have in your life than discipline. The benefits that come as a result of your quest for discipline are extraordinary. But then again, discipline in our time is an extraordinary thing. If more people possessed it, then our world would be a much better place for all of us. Think about it.

We have been spending our lives working hard to achieve our goals because discipline is what drives us. We are self-disciplined which simply means we are focused on our priorities and continue to reinvent ourselves to become our best. We've spent ample time helping and mentoring others because people continually ask for our help. This is why we are writing this book. There are a lot of people who understand what discipline means, but there are a greater percentage of those who don't apply it to their lives whether they grasp the concept or not. We want to help others to teach themselves how to be disciplined through our examples and 85 years of collective experience.

Who is Harris? Harris is truly a unique individual. He is discipline personified. He takes discipline to a whole new level everyday of his life. Always has and always will, that is who he is to the core. It serves him well and he is a success because of it. Always has been and always will be because he's disciplined. Beyond that he is sincere and possesses an extremely caring nature that motivates him to help others succeed in their lives.

Harris travels around the world as a leading IT consultant for Sun Microsystems, has his own publishing company: *Harris Kern's Enterprise Computing Institute* and has authored several books; *Rightsizing the New Enterprise, Managing the New Enterprise, Building the New Enterprise, IT Organization, and Managing IT as an Investment.* In 2001 he also authored his first book on his favorite subject, *Discipline: Six Steps to Unleashing Your Hidden Potential.* But he felt that people still didn't understand how to obtain discipline for themselves. So he began work on this book because he is dedicated to accomplishing his goal of helping others instill this invaluable tool for themselves. He has traveled over 4 million miles as of May 2002. This is a man who does whatever it takes to accomplish his goals. He would like for his past experiences to serve as inspiration for you to reach your own dreams.

I met Harris in 1984 at Fujitsu Microelectronics, Inc., a computer manufacturer headquartered in Santa Clara, CA., where I took a secretarial job in Data Processing with the goal of landing a Computer Operator position to get my feet wet in the computer game. Harris was one of three bosses I worked for there while I started my climb up, but he was without a doubt the most influential mentor I have ever met in my life. Competition in the Silicon Valley was fierce in the 80's and we were worked as hard as we were willing to work. He was constantly pushing me to go above and beyond what my peers were doing so I could move up the ladder quickly and I was all for it.

I had moved from Ohio to meet my goal of working in the computer field with my own hard earned savings and no safety net. I had already set myself apart from most 19 year old women who would never dream of moving across the country away from their family to begin their career. Discipline got me there and after years of planning and hard work fate had me working for Harris. I welcomed the challenge because being financially independent was my goal. I was 20 and Harris was 31 when I began working for him. Managing to keep up with someone who is 11 years my senior and a poster boy for daily marathon-like workouts put my discipline to the test daily. It was no easy feat, there were days when I felt like I was 31 and he was 20 for all his boundless energy and dogged determination. I placed additional pressure on myself because I was young, inexperienced and a woman, which was enough to motivate me to consistently work harder to prove myself and level the playing field with my competition.

Harris barely graduated from high school but he persevered to become a force to be reckoned with in the computer industry. He is one of those people who will always tell it like it is and doesn't mince words. He says what he means and means what he says. Hell hath no fury like Harris when someone is standing between him and a goal!

When I met Harris initially he was just one of the managers that I worked for as a secretary but he struck me as very considerate, methodical and an extremely driven person who never let up. For all his positive attributes he lacked patience. He was not like the other "laid-back" Californians that I worked with at all. He had no tolerance for that attitude whatsoever and he made that abundantly clear. When he gave me a task the due date was and still is "yesterday". Everything was a priority for him and therefore for myself as well. It became routine for me to finish projects early so time never had to be wasted inquiring about their status.

I still remember the day I met with Harris to discuss working part-time as well as overtime to learn about Computer Operations. He was very stern and told me he would expect a lot from me, but that he knew I could handle it because I had already come so far on my own and this was where it would all begin for me. I knew I was capable of whatever I put my mind to, but I couldn't wait to begin my journey with this taskmaster of a boss. I always loved working my butt off for Harris. Why? Because he loved his work and was passionate about making a difference that would benefit everyone. This is something we both felt strongly about. He was constantly raising the bar at every turn and if you didn't jump with him, then you became an obstacle as opposed to a team player. He didn't just manage Operations, he owned it and so did everyone who worked for him. For all the long hours and hard work we put in we were often treated like the bastard stepchildren of the Data Processing Department. But we were the most motivated, reliable, driven bunch of computer geeks you've ever seen! We got noticed. Not just by our Management, but from employees company wide and from our 9 Sales Offices. Our efforts were appreciated. I was able to achieve my own goals as well as those Harris had set out for me and to this day I am amazed at what I was able to accomplish in those few years.

Harris had begun mentoring me from that very first day. We seemed to always be in agreement on ways to tackle problems and our friendship grew as our accomplishments stacked up. I will never forget when I caught a nasty flu bug for about 3 days that kept me worshiping my toilet bowl more often than not. I didn't miss work as a rule, so this was significant. Harris called everyday and by day 3 he asked for directions and brought me the mother of all chicken and rice burritos along with good wishes that I would get better. He made it clear that my health was top priority, but didn't fail to mention that I was missed at work. It was a bit of a commute to my place so this was just another example of his sincerity and willingness to go the extra mile for the sake of others.

I am here to tell you that 14 years later he is the same person when it comes to going the distance to help others and caring about their well being. He caught me completely off guard during a phone call as we were discussing my ideas for my future plans and sharing our opinions on the matter. Out of the blue he asked if we were doing OK financially. At first I was a bit offended that he would think I would ever ask anyone else for money. But I immediately realized and began to remember that this is just the kind of person he is. After all, how many people do you know that would make that offer? It struck me that he has always been that way and continues to be no matter how insanely busy his life is. In spite of his success in his career he is still accessible as a human being. It's that discipline thing.

In 1987 I had gotten engaged to my high school sweetheart who was an Air Force Academy Cadet at the time. Management was pushing me to get into programming or telecommunications since Harris had my hands in all aspects of our department for some time and it was time to move up. I decided I had to leave that job I loved to move to Colorado Springs for my fiancés last 2 years at school before we could be married. I wanted to be 100% sure that we were both truly "meant to be". Harris didn't take the news very well. He had watched me struggle to grow into the independent person he saw in himself who was capable of going the distance. Then I announced that it was time to exchange my career goal for love, which I think is a no-brainer. I took it as a compliment that he believed, as I did, that I could've gone onto much greater things in Silicon Valley. This was a very difficult decision to make. I loved my work and the money was good for a youngster of 23 then, but in the end I felt that my love for my long time friend and fiancé was much stronger and more important than that. You can always find work and make money, but finding someone special enough to share you life with is very difficult.

It was not surprising that I got a job at my new location before my move. I didn't fully appreciate the hoops I had to jump through for Harris until I found out how little most Computer Operators actually do! I thought that sitting in front of the console was what you did in between working data communications, handling customer-related hotline calls, regional sales office problems, being the administrator of critical system management tools, charting equipment upgrades, taking classes, etc., Within months I was promoted to Operations Supervisor of 11 operators and given a promotion. But the job responsibilities were unchallenging, management was weak and I missed that fast-paced world terribly. I was there for 2 years and was being primed once again to jump up to the next level of management but I had to move on to our first Air Force assignment.

The couple times I had contacted Harris over the years to see how he was doing, he "accidentally on purpose" would mention how much fun and excitement I was missing out on. He knew I wanted to know what I had sacrificed, but sometimes the truth hurts. I was always able to tell him that we were very happy and my life of adventure had taken me to many interesting places and various job opportunities. What I didn't tell him was, none provided me with a true passion like the Harris Kern specialized training I had back then. I thrived on the constant stream of challenges.

After a long line of jobs including Civil Service it was time for me to stay at home and do the full-time Mom thing. After working full-time for 13 years, that was quite an experience in itself. Any Mom who has been fortunate enough to be able to choose this option will tell you that the pay sucks but the benefits are immeasurable. I had decided that I was tired of just taking jobs and needed a customized career. Our nomadic military lifestyle is a natural career killer. I loved the opportunity to travel as well as the endless chances to prove myself in a variety of jobs. But I often feared that my nomadic journey to a blissful career might never end. I had set a goal for myself. I was determined once again to find a profession I loved by the time my daughter entered first grade. I had missed that and I deserved to have the same passion for my work that my husband enjoys and I wanted my daughter to see that my passion for family is only one part of me.

My transition time came a year prior to our next move and I needed to figure out what to do with my life. The first order of business was to see if the computer industry was still a viable option. Then I would decide what to do so I could hit the ground running doing something new after we got settled. It was time to locate Harris and get my old mentor's input on the computer scene. I knew he'd have his hands into all kinds of projects and as you can guess, none of that surprised me.

Being the great mentor he is, he gave me his thoughts on the matter and advice that I knew I could count on. A few weeks later he announced that he had written his first non-technical book. He sent me a signed copy and again, this is classic Harris. He could've written this book 20 years ago, but he was busy doing other things he loved. I read it at breakneck speed one evening because it's a quick read to begin with, but I was amazed at the parallels that discipline has played in our lives. I applied a couple of his ideas and my time is spent more efficiently than ever before – my life is better as a result. He felt exactly as I did, set goals in his early teens, met them and continues to set goals today. I began firing off emails telling him relative stories of my life and we concluded that I was the female version of Harris, not nearly as driven by a long shot, but with the very same passion for discipline and mentoring.

It began as a friend wanting to help a friend by sharing thoughts and ideas and seeing areas where Harris' philosophies could be backed up and presented in different ways from a new perspective. Before I knew what hit me I was an editor, website advisor, and last but not least a contributor turned co-author on this book. We have the same vision, but our lives couldn't be more different. Discipline can be applied to everyone's life regardless of age or gender. I was applying discipline at 7 and still do at 37.

What's the moral of our story? If you are disciplined you better watch what you wish for, because you will always get it. If you dare to hitch your wagon to another who lives and breathes discipline then you better hang on, because it's going to be a wild ride!

We want you to make your journey through life the best it can be. People aren't born happy or successful, they have chosen to make these their priorities in life. Past behaviors are history, it's time to focus full throttle on your future goals to enrich your life. Gaining discipline is only as elusive as you allow it to be. Train the mind to manage your life. Play and win the game of your life. After all, it's your life. Live life like you mean it.

We hope you enjoy reading this as much as we have enjoyed writing it for you.

--Karen Willi

PREFACE

Doing More With Less

> "Don't be fooled by the calendar. There are only as many days in the year as you make use of. One man gets only a week's value out of a year while another man gets a full year's value out of a week."
> Charles Richards

Each day has become a substantial challenge for the young and elderly alike. Whether you're 19 years old (school, fulltime job, social activities, etc.) or if you're in your early 70's like our Moms (household CEO, part time job, grandkids, cook, etc.) there are never enough hours in a day to finish your daily activities. All that time is spent just maintaining your current lifestyle. Consequently many of your daily chores and responsibilities get pushed over into the next day. What about new goals and objectives? Forget it - who has the time? You're always trying to play catch-up instead of getting ahead of the game. You've become a slave to your daily routine.

The pressure is all around us, from the business world to our home life. Our society goes non-stop. At work management is cutting back everywhere except on the workload. Corporations are getting mean and lean by cutting back on the number of employees. The job functions are still the same, but your employer hasn't cut back on your responsibilities, yet you're expected to pick up the slack. This seems to be the common theme these days. Accomplishing more with less time and resources has become the norm for all of us.

At home both adults are usually working. The kids want your time – you have to eat – someone has to cook – so nighttime consists of surfing the Internet, doing email, or whatever. In addition, oh yes, we almost forgot, you would really like to exercise on a regular basis. Something has to give. Like it or not, the pressure will only get worse. The only way to get ahead is to continuously motivate yourself everyday to drive and push yourself like never before. But, that's easier said than done.

Your body will need to be in superb physical condition. Whether you like it or not you won't have a choice but to cut back on some of the simple pleasures life has to offer (i.e. sleeping a full 8 hours, watch football all day on Sundays, or sitting around doing nothing). Work will not let up, and neither will the kids. Will it ever get better? No. It will not. Industry competition and economics will continue to push the employer to get more out of their employees. Doing more with less is now a way of life. Whether it's at home or work you have no choice.

At the time of this writing Harris was traveling a half million miles a year (for the past six years) while running two businesses, exercising 7 days a week, and spending time with his wife and kids. He made a choice and at the age of 48 he still wanted more out of life.

> "Don't be afraid your life will end; be afraid that it
> will never begin."
> Grace Hanson

As Harris travels the globe meeting thousands of people a year, it's frightening to see how many individuals can't get ahead in life. Most of them want to accomplish more than they currently do. Some of the most common remarks are:

> ➢ *"I have limited bandwidth"*
> ➢ *"It's hard enough just maintaining my current lifestyle"*
> ➢ *"There aren't enough hours in a day"*
> ➢ *"I'm too tired at the end of the day"*

People Are Not Excelling

Why are people having a hard time managing their professional and personal life? Never mind trying to excel, it's hard enough for people just to keep up with things and maintain their current lifestyle. In this day and age of everything being on Internet time status quo will lead to failure whether it's work or in your personal life, failure will be imminent. We need to do more with less time just to survive. Whether you're trying to get ahead and accomplish as much as possible, or just trying to balance your personal time and career, discipline will be your only hope for success.

In order to excel there needs to be change. Change in the way people currently live their lives (i.e., work, sleep, play, eat, etc.). You name it-it <u>all</u> has to change. It's really a shame if you don't make a concerted effort to change, because all of us are born with the potential but unfortunately that power will stay dormant with the majority of people.

We believe there <u>are</u> enough hours in a day. The problem is most people don't manage their time effectively. To become successful or just to keep your head above water you need to manage every minute of your life. Unfavorable as it may sound you will have no choice but to structure your life as if you were a supervisor with 50 employees managing their 8-hour workdays.

> "Most people live and die
> with their music still unplayed.
> They never dare to try."
> *Mary Kay Ash*

Self-help books usually provide you with the 'how-to' but don't provide you with a proven method for continuous self-motivation. Motivational speeches only pump you up for a few hours or maybe a couple days if they're extraordinarily good speakers. New Year's resolutions are nothing but hot air because they are empty promises based solely on a date on the calendar. Most people just don't do a very good job of managing their personal life. They would falter on their goals and objectives, change their priorities on the fly, commit to people and never follow through, etc. For us and we're hoping for you as well, life is all about accomplishments. They could be learning something new, working towards a promotion, buying your first home, balancing your life so you're committed to spending a set number of hours with your family each week, etc. Nothing is more rewarding than feeling like you've gone through a week or an entire month keeping all your commitments and accomplishing important milestones. Wouldn't it be great to feel that way for an entire year or even better, the rest of your life?

> "Every man dies. Not every man lives."
> *Brauchear*

In the first book, *Discipline: Six Steps to Unleashing Your Hidden Potential*, the importance of discipline is discussed & the six simple steps it takes to acquire discipline are given. Throughout the book, the image of a person opening a door and through the door seeing a reflection of him or herself in a mirror is referenced. This is an image called upon again and again because it symbolizes the relationship Harris built with himself in the years it took to acquire discipline. It was all about fulfilling a contract with himself. The book is about you and the constant struggle you have with yourself to fulfill that same promise. If you step through that door and don't like what you see in the mirror, then the book can help you develop the discipline to enjoy stepping through that door rather than dreading it. It's a daily battle as you seek out that elusive element to balancing home and career, personal time and family, and the other forces that life hurls at you on a daily basis.

> "One can never consent to creep when one feels
> an impulse to soar."
> *Helen Keller*

The goal was to write a very simple book with a very simple message. The book could be read by anyone at any age. In very little time the reader will quickly understand the steps necessary to acquire discipline. We all know how important discipline is and always will be. So why don't people do a better job of applying it to enhance and organize their lives to get as much accomplished as humanly possible each and everyday?

Harris thought his objectives were accomplished. The sole purpose for writing that book was to not only teach people about discipline but to help them acquire it as well. You might say that accomplishing one out of two goals isn't bad, but Harris felt that he hadn't completed that goal in its entirety. People were still asking me the same questions after the first book was published.

> ➢ *Why is it so difficult to put some structure in my life?*
> ➢ *Why is it so hard to focus on my priorities?*
> ➢ *Why can't I be consistent with my exercise?*
> ➢ *There aren't enough hours in a day to do everything – I have so much I want to accomplish and I can't keep up with it all!*
> ➢ *I can't motivate myself – I need a push.*

Harris says, "At first I was perplexed because I thought I was preaching discipline 101. In my mind this stuff was easy to comprehend. It wasn't rocket science. So what's up with these people? Why couldn't they get their act together?

After hearing these above statements I realized that understanding the steps for acquiring discipline and learning how to acquire it is one thing and *doing it* is something else altogether. Attempting to practice it consistently is where people normally fail. Therefore, the guiding principle behind this book is helping people motivate and push themselves by training their mind. Our goal for this book is to teach people how to acquire discipline for themselves."

This book is about **training the mind** so you can use it as a tool to manage your life as if it were a business. This is the business end of what it takes to get your life headed in the direction that you want it to go. You will learn how to train your mind and what the power of a trained mind can do for you. As with the first book, this will also be very easy to read, absorb, and comprehend.

"Don't go through Life, Grow through Life."
Eric Butterworth

Discipline is the one thing that encompasses all the positive aspects of ourselves in order to remove all those undesirable things that challenge all of us everyday of our lives. This is why all those self-help books that target specific areas (losing weight, building confidence, career enhancement) are gathering dust and you are still searching for some divine intervention to come into your life. You're holding it in your hands right now. You know its true. Take a minute and think about it. For everything that you have struggled to overcome in your life the reason it remains an issue is a simple lack of discipline to pull it off. Don't be fooled. There is nothing simple about it, but it remains the one single attribute that stands between you and your goals. If you had discipline you never would have felt so overwhelmed by so many things - ever. Lack of it has kept you from applying all those previous readings to your life.

This book is for anyone who is tired of battling the same old bothersome issues in their life and knows they can beat them. It doesn't matter how many issues stand in your way, even one is too many once you welcome discipline into your life. We don't just tell you how to apply it, we show you. You will build your own Personally Regulated Improvement Model to Excel (PRIME) to incorporate discipline into your own life and on your own terms. You have complete control of it. Once you've successfully PRIMEd your life, you can use that control to enhance the quality of your life any way you please.

DEDICATION

> "Life is what we make it. Always has been.
> Always will be."
> *Grandma Moses*

We've been working for years training the mind and body to function simultaneously for maximum production. Our driving force in writing this book is our desire to help others make the very best of their lives as we have through sheer discipline.

Because of our disciplined nature we refuse to give up trying to help people overcome some of their shortcomings, which impede them from achieving many accomplishments. For us accomplishments are what life is all about. A complete life is one that is filled with many major accomplishments. It's a life that's structured, organized, committed and takes full advantage of every minute of the day.

We want you to realize your full potential on your own terms by applying discipline in every facet of your life. There is nothing more rewarding than sharing a life altering formula with others who can benefit from it as we have.

> "Those who dream by night in the dusty re   ses
> of their minds wake in the day to find that
> vanity; but the dreamers of the day are
> dangerous people for they may act their dream
> with open eyes, and make it possible."
> *Lawrence of Arabia*

Dare to be a daydreamer. Then use your mind to make those dreams come true for yourself once and for all. Don't dwell on the dream; focus on creating your reality. It's your life. Live it to it's fullest and strive to be your best. Can you afford to waste your precious time being unfulfilled or unhappy? We don't think so. And who would want to?

Do you continually ask yourself any of the following questions time and again: Is there more to life? Is this really what I was born to be doing for the rest of my life? I had so many plans but how can I possibly do any of these things at my age? If any of these sound familiar then it's time to start asking yourself, why not?

> "If not now, when?"
> --- *The Talmud*

ACKNOWLEDGEMENTS

Harris' Acknowledgments:

I am grateful to my friend and colleague Rich Schiesser for allowing me to tap into his brilliant mind. I have a lot of respect for his intelligence and sincerity. He was particularly helpful with the chapter on PRIME.

To Mayra Muniz for her partnership, friendship, loyalty, and support. Special thanks for her timely and valuable feedback on the overall content, graphics design and providing key editorial contributions. Most of all I would like to thank her for adapting to my <u>relentless</u> characteristic.

To my mom for simply being the greatest human being on this planet.

To my friends Eve, Paul, Scott, and Sid for making my mornings entertaining.

To Jenny Mittlestat for her friendship, support and editorial contributions. Jenny has become a truly wonderful friend and someone I respect and admire.

Last but certainly not least, it's a pleasure to acknowledge my good friend and co-author Karen for her many contributions. Her tireless effort and countless enhancements during the development and editorial process were truly inspiring. Thank you for coming back into my life!

Karen's Acknowledgments:

To my best friend and husband, Bernie, for reading every word of our manuscripts time and again and giving his valuable input and always useful editorial contributions. For his love, support, encouragement and patience during this entire process. Last but not least, for allowing me to monopolize the computer while his much-loved flight simulator games gathered dust; and he lived to tell about it. I'm a very lucky woman.

To my daughter, Alexa, for her love in the form of those brief and silent hugs and kisses while I'm writing. For her wonderful encouragement that has caused an immediate need for a scrapbook to house the beautiful collection of personalized bookmarks, notes of support and confidence that I will always treasure. You are, without a doubt, the accomplishment that I am most proud of.

To my dear brother and friend Phil, who was the first mentor in my life who went out of his way to spend time with me and fortunately for me, he still does. You are a natural-born teacher and the world is a better place because you are in it. Your words of encouragement have always meant the world to me and your support in this endeavor is no different. I am forever grateful for your friendship, love and support.

I'm grateful for my Mom, Dorothy. Without her, these words could not have been written. She is responsible for taking every opportunity to teach me discipline from day one. Mom, my favorite line is still " I can handle it". I am in awe of her accomplishments and am inspired by her incredible strength, love and determination. Your infectious positive attitude, sense of humor and beautiful smile are gifts that I cherish everyday of my life. This isn't the first time I've surprised you and it won't be the last.

Last but not least to Harris, my mentor and trusted friend, for giving me the opportunity and privilege of writing this book with you. I'm grateful that you gave me absolute freedom to take it wherever it led me. You're a fearless man! It's good to be back on a new venture that I love once again and I thank you for leading me to it. Of all your accomplishments, I believe that mentoring is not only what you do best but it's what you were born to do. You must never stop.

1.   INTRODUCTION

Life Is All About Accomplishments

"Life has a practice of living you, if you don't live it."
Philip Larkin

When are people going to realize that as far as we know we're all on this planet for one time and one time only? There are no second chances. We continually ask ourselves; why are millions of people wasting so much time everyday? We can't imagine not accomplishing one goal after another (major and minor) until the day we drop. If there are no accomplishments, there is no life, or at best it's an unfulfilled life. There is no purpose for living. You may exist, but that's not living. Living is progressing, not merely breathing.

"To live is so startling it leaves little time for anything else."
Emily Dickinson

There is no greater feeling in the world than accomplishing a major goal. Once you complete a goal you will never forget it. It's hard to describe in mere words what the feeling is like. It's a kind of euphoria that not only makes you feel invincible, but is extremely addictive as well. The level of intensity is relative to the difficulty of the goal. The harder the goal, the stronger the "feeling of accomplishment" will be. You can take our word for it. We still remember each and every goal, even the ones we accomplished over 30 years ago.

To us life is about accomplishments and feeling on top of the world each time you've achieved one. What a rush, one after another, like no other feeling. Those are REAL highs. It's a self-inflicted adrenaline rush that you can't get out of your system once you've experienced it. The more you accomplish, the more you crave more accomplishments for yourself. You will never be satisfied. What a feeling it is to always want more and have that hunger to take on new challenges and to accomplish more year after year. Life now has purpose.

1

HARRIS KERN / KAREN WILLI

A World of Hurt

"It may seem to be conceited to suppose that you can do anything important toward improving the lot of mankind. But this is a fallacy. You must believe that you can help bring about a better world. A good society is produced only by good individuals, just as truly as a majority in a presidential election is produced by the votes of single electors. Everybody can do something toward creating in his own environment kindly feelings rather than anger, reasonableness rather than hysteria, happiness rather than misery."

Bertrand Russel

Karen writes: What is this world coming to? What is so lacking in our society that makes us so dependent on security systems for our homes, cars and every other facet of our lives? Why can't we trust anyone anymore? Why are school shootings happening all over the world? Employees are "going postal" in their workplaces. If we don't feel safe at work and our children are fearful at school and we come home and have to punch in an access code just to enter our own homes then we think there are a lot of things very disturbing and awfully wrong about all of this. Prisons are at full capacity. Do you ever wonder where offenders go or how many are "let go" when they shouldn't be because of overcrowded prisons? We've got road rage happening just about everywhere. You have to lock your car doors for fear of getting car jacked at any time of the day or night. People who live in exclusive neighborhoods are always "surprised" when any kind of crime or graffiti shows up in their neck of the woods. For some odd reason we think if we spend more of our hard earned money we will be able to live in a gated community with impenetrable security, as opposed to our last place where security was only sufficient. You've heard this stuff on the news. You already know it's a frightening and sad fact of life. These gut-wrenching things are happening and we sit feeling helpless watching it on the news or worse yet, dealing with some form of it in our own lives. We think prevention is always the best option. That's what this book can provide if you take it seriously. It could mean a better future for all of us, especially our children. It needs to start now because things certainly aren't getting better.

3

It's discipline, plain and simple. Lack of discipline is rampant and we're not just talking about in urban areas. Generations before us didn't know how fortunate they were to have had so little to occupy their lives other than their livelihoods. Talk about a true example of irony. They were farmers, factory workers, coal miners, soldiers; you name any job that you couldn't imagine doing even for one day, let alone a lifetime. All this was done in the poorest working conditions that were just accepted as part of the job. Most occupations required hard physical and mental labor from sunrise to sunset; that was what they did because they had to survive. Virtually everyone was busting their ass just to put food on the table for their families. The word "whiner" wasn't used because there were none. Building a country isn't easy and that is what it took to get us where we are today. It was built from the ground up. Herein lies the problem. You can't appreciate what you haven't experienced for yourself. Those of us fortunate enough to live in our advanced society that was built on hard working individuals have no appreciation for it.

When you have no option but to work hard, discipline is instilled as a habit. There is no "free time" and if there is you can bet it is spent doing something fun to relieve the stress of the day. Certainly not wasted getting into trouble with the law because your punishment from your parents would've involved opening a huge old can of whoop ass on your sorry self! And if those parents didn't do it, "the look" would've been enough to set you straight from everyone else you knew because in those days "the look" was used and respected as a formidable discipline tool. This is where you learn that you don't mess with hard-working individuals. Punishment was swift and painful so those foolish enough to repeat their misconduct clearly weren't the "sharpest tools in the shed". There was never a time or place where bad or disrespectful behavior was tolerated. Things sure have changed haven't they? It doesn't have to be this way.

We are afforded more time and money to work in any kind of occupation of our choosing because employment is not limited to back breaking work anymore. It is anything but that in most cases. Because we tend to live in cities where employment is plentiful, we don't have that sprawling farm in the country that we sometimes dream of. Growing up on a farm is a great way to raise children because everyone has chores to do that needs attention on a daily basis. When everyone is busy the entire family sleeps better, has less time for fighting and learns that every job - no matter how small - contributes to the big picture in the end. It's discipline 101, but its every single day 24/7/365. I'll be the first to admit that I didn't fully appreciate it growing up, but now the experience is something I treasure. My Mom grew up on a dairy farm so she was a master at making hard work look easy. "If you want to have your own horses, then you're going to have to shovel some shit" she used to say. We all have to shovel loads of it in our lives in many forms, but most of us - if given the choice, will give up the horse because we refuse to work hard for those things we dream of having. We're lazy. I have never been afraid of hard work and as a rule I chose it more often than not. It's that sense of accomplishment that keeps you looking for more challenges to outdo yourself.

These days, parents are often times both working outside the home, leaving kids at daycare for someone else to discipline - with no other option, driving them to all their activities to accommodate "giving them something to do so they don't get into trouble" which adds more stress to everyone's already hectic schedules. The farms with the upgraded discipline package built-in are dwindling. This is where we are today. These are the cards we've been dealt. We must manage our lives to the minute.

If you haven't learned discipline in childhood then you need to learn it now so you can realize the benefits for yourself. Don't you think we'd all be better off if every parent caught a ride on the discipline clue bus before they had kids? The sooner, the better we think. When my husband and I were still childless I used to joke that every married couple should get a dog and discipline it together as a precursor to having kids. We actually put this to the test and I'm here to tell you it's a real eye opener. See who ends up taking the dog outside more often and who prefers playtime to the actual training process. This animal will become your first child and the similarities to actual parenting styles are right on the money. If you're both having trouble making time to discipline your dog before you have kids, then exactly who is going to be finding time for that unruly dog and your new baby?

Why discipline your dog in the first place? So it can be trained to behave in society among other people and animals so it's happy and healthy and can be the best dog it can be! That's why. Have you noticed how many dog-mauling cases have occurred in recent years? If the owners of those poor animals would take the time to discipline them or have the discipline to know what a particular breed is capable of we wouldn't have this problem. My own dog is more disciplined than some people. This is a sad statement, but it is brutally honest. She happily asks to run outside every morning to fetch our paper for us, runs back inside, drops it at our feet and waits for her reward. Sure, we trained her and yes it took a bit of time as a puppy but she's been doing that for 10 years without fail. If my dog could talk, she would tell you that discipline is fun, rewarding, gives her purpose, keeps her fit, and she draws attention and receives accolades everywhere she goes because of it. What more could a dog want out of life? Pretty smart for a dog, you have to admit.

5

Why do you think most parents are so proud when their kids choose to serve their country in the military? Yeah, there's the pride thing, but the first thought is "finally that kid is going to get some discipline!" What's up with that? Didn't this person live with you for the last 18 years and weren't you responsible for their upbringing? We've got news for you. There are plenty of undisciplined people in the armed forces. It's a golden opportunity to learn discipline, but not everyone takes the ball and runs with it. Most take the free education and run like greyhounds to the nearest exit to a life chock full of mediocrity because it's "not for them". It's really not for everyone. Discipline means sacrifice and the military is all about that. What matters most is that you get a taste of it and build on the discipline you've achieved. It's not just about making it through basic training, it's about pushing yourself to new levels everyday and applying it to your life. For those who allow themselves to be disciplined, they will be rewarded in ways they never could've imagined.

I am temporarily living in San Diego, California which is hands down the choicest assignment that we have had and possibly ever will have in my husband's entire Air Force career. While thumbing through a Naval Station phone book I saw a listing for the Naval Discipline Barracks. I called them inquiring about their function and how it worked because of its relevance to this book. I got the old "I'm going to have to refer you to the Legal Office Ma'am" routine. Yes, discipline is such a cruelty that they wouldn't want to say anything that "civilians" might see as harsh punishment. I spoke with a representative of the Discipline Barracks Legal office who said, "If someone is in need of discipline this is where he or she is sent to get it. They are restricted to that dorm at all times, but they are expected to work their normal duty day. Their entire schedule is set for them; when they wake up, when and where they eat, everything they do until they have done their time which is relative to the offense." Discipline yourself, or have it done for you. What a country! I'm sure the parents of those dorm rats who are getting their daily dose of "Vitamin D" shoved down their throats are not surprised that "additional training" became necessary. That pill would have been much easier to swallow given in small doses at opportune moments throughout childhood. Would've saved a lot of people an awful lot of time, money, embarrassment and humiliation that will last a lifetime.

These are all things that none of us should have in the back or the front of our minds every minute of everyday. We are eternal optimists. We know things can always be better. This is why we believe that what follows in these pages is paramount for our future. It's not all bleak because there are an awful lot of people who are disciplined and they are doing all the right things. We think we need more of them, a lot more. Our team is in dire need of players and it's time we launched a recruiting campaign to reach this goal. The quality of our

6

lives depends on it. Everyone agrees that making this world a better place is something that will keep millions of us gainfully employed for generations to come. All we are trying to do is to make discipline a household word once again. That's it! To shock you into the realization that this is the critical element that is missing from our lives and it can be learned. It is important for you as a person, your children, society, and generations to come. One disciplined person can make all the difference in the world. Unfortunately – so can one who is not disciplined."

You Have The Power

> "I was always looking outside myself for Strength and confidence but it comes from within.
> It is there all the time."
> *Anna Freud*

Do you really like what you see in the mirror? Are you happy with your current lifestyle? Would you like your life to be a bit more organized? Wouldn't you like to have a few extra hours at the end of each week? Would you like to be motivated everyday of the year? Do you wish you could be consistent with your priorities? Do you wish you could be sincere about your commitments? Do you wish these questions would end? We're sure you answered yes to all of these questions. You have the power to build these characteristics and others that are equally important. Being disciplined is not hereditary; it comes with hard work.

You have the power to make what you want out of your life. Make your life challenging and excitement will naturally follow. Life is so precious. Why waste it? Live it – come on, we know it sounds like a cliché but "Be all you can be." So get on it, what are you waiting for? If you refuse to accept anything but the best, you'll always get the best. Begin to live life as you wish to live. You have no idea how much power your mind and body possess, if trained properly you can take on anything. Never underestimate the power of your mind.

Age Has Nothing To Do With It

> "Age is of no importance unless you are a cheese."
> Billy Burke

Harris writes: It doesn't matter if you're 13 or 53 years old; age is no excuse for not having discipline in your life. It really gets on my nerves when people say; "my son is too young – I'll wait until he's a teenager" or "I'm 45 – I'm too old to become disciplined or I've been UN-disciplined all my life". It's <u>never</u> too late or too early to make something out of your life.

My son is 8 years old and I've already started mentoring him in one of the most important aspects of discipline; taking care of his body. I live in Los Angeles and my son Kevin lives in San Francisco with my former wife. I visit with him several times a month and he stays overnight in the same hotel with me. The hotel has a well-equipped gym, which I use frequently. I've been waiting for the right time to get Kevin involved with some form of exercise. Recently he's been telling me that he wants to have "big muscles like daddy". These words were music to my ears. My only concern with bringing him into the gym at this age was that he wouldn't like it. That's because society has been brainwashing us for years by saying "it's not healthy for kids, especially at such a tender age of 8." I have a different opinion. If you start children out slowly and cautiously there won't be any health risks. Although my son's goal was to have big muscles, my goal for him went much deeper than that. I wanted to train his mind as well as his body in making exercise fun and part of his normal routine. My objective was for him to ask me to go and exercise with him. I did not want to force him into it. He had to want it for himself. My other concern was that he might get bored. You know how kids are at that age; boredom sets in quickly. I knew once he was in the gym I had 30 minutes of quality time to train him. I started him out by showing him how to walk and then run on the treadmill, we did some sit ups together and I showed him how to use a few of the weight machines (with no poundage). We exercised for about 30 minutes together – he loved it – he's starting to learn about discipline and we're spending some quality time together. Now he wants to go all the time.

Kevin is just beginning to learn about one of the key ingredients for acquiring discipline. Hopefully he will continue to ask me to exercise with him. I will continue to play mind games with him i.e., when we walk by the gym I'll say, "Hey look Kevin, the gym is empty do you want to go in there and play on the tread mill?" So far it's been working. There is no playing but I make it feel that way to him. I will even tune the TV to Nickelodeon while he's running on the treadmill. He loves it-and that's half the battle of achieving anything that matters in life. Make it fun – at any age.

Sid, a friend of mine, is 60 years old, retired and is in the gym every morning at 4:30 a.m. like clockwork for a 2-hour workout. During the day he does volunteer work. His workday starts at 7:30 a.m. He never misses a beat. He exercises and works regardless of any obstacles that come along. He is extremely committed and dedicated to his exercise routine and his volunteer work. Sid also has goals and is a very devoted family man. Although he's retired Sid keeps his mind and body extremely active. He has many goals still left to accomplish. He is the picture of health and is what we all should aspire to when we retire. The truth is, he puts most men half his age to shame. Being a role model is never easy, but then again, if it were we'd have a lot more of them.

> ## "It is never too late to be what you might have been."
> *George Eliot*

Status Quo is Failure

> ## "Life has a practice of living you, if you don't live it."
> *Philip Larkin*

What's the point of going through an entire lifetime doing the same thing? I'm talking about the same routine day in and day out i.e., commute, work & commute, home etc., you know, lather, rinse, repeat... What a waste of precious time! We all have certain chores and responsibilities everyday but life is so much more than that.

If you define life as: Getting up around 7 a.m., going to work, coming home at 6pm, watching TV for a few hours, and going to sleep - in other words, the same old boring routine Monday – Friday then your current lifestyle is failure in our book. If complacency is your cup of tea then, your current lifestyle is a waste of your livelihood. You are capable of getting so much more out of life and we're sure you don't need us to tell you that. Your life needs to change and this book will help you do just that.

> "Do more than is required. What is the distance between someone who achieves their goals consistently and those who spend their lives and careers merely following? The extra mile."
> *Gary Ryan Blair*

While you're living on this planet - you must <u>always</u> do the things that you never dreamt possible. Things you felt were out of your league or that you didn't have the talent to do or things that you weren't qualified to do-you MUST do. Challenges make life worthwhile and exciting, but talking about it and actually doing something about it are two different ball games. Attempting to do it without incorporating it into your Personally Regulated Improvement Model to Excel (PRIME – see chapter 2) will constitute failure. You can do anything as long as you are committed, you have passion behind it and it's properly documented (in your mind) with associated goals and priorities. Time is passing you by. How much time can you afford to let pass before you start excelling in life?

Don't Wait Until Tomorrow

> "Tomorrow life is too late; live today."
> *--Martial*

Why are people always procrastinating or putting things off until the next day/month/year? That's an easy one to answer. People look at time as a plentiful resource (there's plenty of it, so what's the urgency?) instead of seeing it as the valuable and scarce commodity that it is. Every minute (not hour) is valuable and precious and once wasted it will never come back into your life. Once you start believing that, you will begin to manage time efficiently as you would manage a special project at work. Most of us waste so much time each day that by the end of the day you've run out of time to get everything accomplished so it's put off till the next day, week, or whenever. But if time is managed properly, you will have the extra time to complete the things you want to on any given day.

"I recommend you to take care of the minutes,
for the hours will take care of themselves."
Lord Chesterfield

People ask us; "Isn't it difficult to manage every minute of every day? Isn't that too stressful? My life is already way too hectic and unmanageable." All we're emphasizing (see chapter 2) is that people do have the time – they just don't manage it very well.

2. PERSONALLY REGULATED IMPROVEMENT MODEL TO EXCEL

> *"If you want to make good use of your time,*
> *you've got to know what's most important and*
> *then give it all you've got."*
> *Lee Iacocca*

Every new business starts with a business plan. The business plan provides them with a roadmap on how to effectively expand and manage their business. With a plan there's focus, but without focus there's limited potential or often times failure. Successful companies don't try to conquer the world. They focus on their business plan, which highlights their core competencies.

> *"Failing to plan is planning to fail."*
> *Effie Jones*

We recommend you do the same with your life. Build a Personally Regulated Improvement Model to Excel (PRIME) to start acquiring discipline and to effectively manage your life. When developing your PRIME don't try to take on the world in the beginning or you might set yourself up for failure. Stick to goals that are achievable so you can start gaining some confidence to embark on the more challenging ones. As you begin to gain confidence, then you can stretch yourself a little bit at a time.

> *"If you have built castles in the air,*
> *your work need not be lost;*
> *that is where they should be.*
> *Now put the foundations under them."*
> *Henry David Thoreau*

Documenting your PRIME to acquire discipline is simple. The difficult part is motivating and pushing yourself each and everyday. The only way to motivate yourself everyday is by training your mind (see chapter 6) until everything becomes automatic. When you are functioning within the parameters of your PRIME it will seem as if there's hardly any effort on your part.

The plan (PRIME) to manage your life includes the following steps:

1. <u>Analyzing your current daily routine</u>:

It's imperative to start out by documenting your current routine. What exactly do you do in a 24-hour period? This is by no means a brief description but a very detailed outline of what you do with <u>every</u> minute in a 24-hour period.

It begins from the moment the alarm goes off in the morning. It includes the times you spend hitting the snooze button and total elapsed time until you wake up and are vertical. Every minute needs to be documented; your commute to work, how long you shower, how long you watch TV on the weekdays and weekends, etc. In the section titled: Your Current Routine we provide you with some examples of how we documented someone's schedule.

2. <u>Addressing your weaknesses and obstacles</u>:

> "If you listen to your fears, you will die never knowing what a great person you might have been."
> *Robert A. Schuller*

It's one thing to document your weaknesses and obstacles but you also need to establish an action plan to address them. Whether it's being afraid to speak in front of an audience, fear of heights, or lack of courage, etc. you need to address these issues. If you don't they'll rear their ugly head when you least expect it, especially as you're trying to accomplish your goals. If you don't have an action plan to address them then you'll never acquire discipline.

3. <u>Establishing goals with milestones</u>:

> "People with goals succeed because they know where they are going."
> *Earl Nightingale*

Of all six steps this is probably the easiest. Anyone can write down or memorize a few goals. Unfortunately, we all know that only a small percentage of people ever complete them. Goals should <u>never</u> be written down unless you have had success with this method in the past or if this works best for you. For most people this is ineffective. That little piece of paper will either get lost or just sit around gathering dust. If you memorize those goals you'll always be thinking of them.

It's important to differentiate between *major* and *minor* goals and to get the right combination of both. What is the difference between them? That is for you to decide: You establish the guidelines. Everyone is different. You have to consider the complexity, magnitude, and your current lifestyle before deciding which goals are minor and which ones are major.

Examples of major and minor goals are explained in detail in my first book titled *Discipline: Six Steps to Unleashing Your Hidden Potential.*

Think of goals in this way:

> ➢ *How long will it take to accomplish it?*
> ➢ *What will I have to sacrifice?*
> ➢ *What other areas of my life will this impact?*
> ➢ *Do I have a prayer of ever accomplishing this?*

You can never have goals that depend on someone else. There are no partnerships here. Placing dependencies on goals is never a good idea and will surely lead to failure. You must own the goal in its entirety.

When establishing your goals, make sure there's plenty of passion and enthusiasm behind each one. Without passion you'll never complete the goal. Each goal has to hold a special meaning for you. It cannot be just another goal for the sake of having one. You have to embrace each and every goal.

> **"Nothing great in the world has ever been accomplished without passion."**
> G.W.F. Hegel

Just writing down goals won't get the job done. For each goal there has to be associated milestones with dates (see Table 2.1 below).

Table 2.1: Milestones

	Completion Date	Milestones
Exercise every day of the week in one year's time (Currently 2002).	3/1/2003	➤ Consistently exercise 3 days a week
	6/1/2003	➤ Consistently exercise 5 days a week
	10/1/2003	➤ Consistently exercise everyday of the week

Goals without milestones and dates are empty words and gestures and ultimately a waste of time. If you only occasionally think about your goals (once a week or monthly), you will not be successful.

4. Establishing Backup Plans:

"The majority of men meet with failure because of their lack of persistence in creating new plans to take the place of those which fail."
Napoleon Hill

Every goal should have several different options to attain successful completion. Always have a backup plan. Always keep those wheels in motion by thinking of smarter and easier ways to complete goals ahead of schedule. As mentioned previously, goals are not an afterthought. Articulating plans to complete them ahead of schedule needs to be a constant endeavor. Those plans need to be developed into minor goals and tracked rigorously. These minor goals may change frequently to assist you in completing your primary goals.

5. Establishing priorities:

"Once you have mastered time, you will
understand how true it is that most people
overestimate what they can accomplish in a
year—and underestimate what they can achieve
in a decade!"
Anthony Robbins

In order to accomplish these newly established goals, you're life needs to be prioritized. These priorities will help you accomplish your goals. These are your guidelines plain and simple. There's no veering off course. If you stray, you will NEVER accomplish your goals. The most important aspect of acquiring discipline is prioritizing your current lifestyle. After establishing goals, you need to set priorities.

Priorities should not become a total burden on your lifestyle. Remember life's unexpected surprises. Those obstacles and roadblocks can wreak havoc on your priorities. Look ahead and hope for the best but always plan for the worst. You must adhere to these priorities regardless of anything else you do at all costs, until you have achieved discipline. These priorities must be followed daily. They should actually become part of your normal routine. Always stay focused on them no matter what the situation or whatever the predicament.

Priorities are a set of objectives. These objectives are usually lumped up into categories. Table 2.2 below highlights some objectives and their associated categories.

Table 2.2: Prioritize Objectives

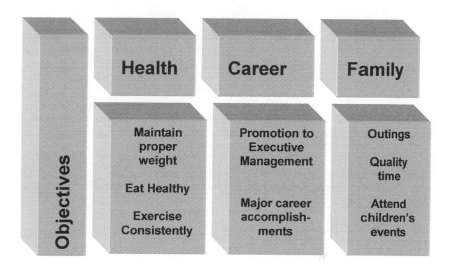

Harris says, "I set only two priorities. Anything else I accomplished was a bonus, because I knew that there would be days when I could adhere to only two."

6. <u>Establishing a new (formal) daily routine</u>:

Based on your newly established goals and priorities it's time to document your new daily routine (see the section titled: My Current Routine for examples). Every minute is now accounted for. If you really want to acquire discipline strictly adhere to your new schedule.

Harris writes: It may sound like I want people to turn into robots or machines. In a sense, yes, but this is a <u>good</u> thing! This is in order to get your mind and body working together to achieve discipline. I've been programming my mind and body for maximum production. Many times I've been labeled as a robot or machine. There are certainly negative connotations associated with being called a machine, but it depends on your point of view. Webster's Dictionary defines a robot: *"A machine that looks like a human and performs various complex acts."* I consider this to be a great compliment to my unwavering commitment to my goals.

Karen writes: Harris' robot or machine label is my Martha Stewart label. Because I'm a woman who enjoys going the extra mile when it comes to taking care of my family as well as diving headfirst into my work I've been branded with this one from my friends. It's both humorous and complimentary because it's always coupled with other compliments. Both Harris and I have heard many of our bosses make comments to this affect; "You do more work in one day than I can get out of anyone else in a week, or if more people worked as hard as you my job would be a lot easier!"

These somewhat negatively charged labels prove that our discipline is something that everyone else thinks is totally unobtainable or completely out of reach for them. The fact that so many people think discipline is abnormal speaks volumes about the current state of our society. When others believe that they could never be disciplined themselves, this is typically when anti-compliments start flying. They're jealous, plain and simple. I'm no Martha and Harris is no machine. But we both believe very strongly about the tremendous impact discipline has played in our lives.

It's Not a Team Event

> "Our business in life is not to get ahead of others but to get ahead of ourselves – to break our own records, to outstrip our yesterdays by our today, to do our work with more force than before."
> *Stewart B. Johnson*

Acquiring discipline isn't a team event. It's an individual effort for life. Your mission is to continually outperform in every facet of life. We're born alone, we die alone and in between we should spend our lives striving to be the best we can be. We should do it for ourselves first and for everyone else second. No one is perfect. That's why each and every one of us has so much to learn in order to achieve our own idea of "perfection". This learning process is called life. Our plan for reaching the summit of "perfection" is to apply discipline to every aspect of my life. It's just about being your best. As long as we know we've given our best effort everyday we are never disappointed. On the other hand, if we're disappointed we know that we didn't apply discipline or that goal wouldn't have slipped through our fingers. Our fate is our own and we take full responsibility for it.

No one else can make you a better person. You can learn through the examples and mistakes of others, but you must learn for yourself and use that knowledge to enhance your own life. You have to take your life's lessons when and wherever they present themselves. Life hands you opportunities everyday. They come in two forms, opportunities to learn and opportunities to teach. If you utilize each one of these moments you will be constantly learning and helping others simultaneously. It becomes a habit that is unbreakable, not that you'd ever want to break it anyway. In other words, if you're constantly learning and teaching then your life will be very full and rewarding and you'll be a better person for it. Be a sponge and soak up everything you observe in your daily life. Tomorrow you'll be a better person – always.

You shouldn't depend on others as a rule. We know we can count on ourselves to make things happen. Those few times we've relied on others seem to end in disappointment more often than not. Being independent is what drives us. Watching others be dependent on everyone else is what drives us crazy. We're convinced that some people could not exist very long without the endless stream of assistance they get from those around them. Those they depend on are enablers and the best thing they could do is to break this cycle, otherwise it will never end. What becomes of them when they lose those they rely on so heavily? There's nothing wrong with having a support network for stressful times. The problem is; Dependent people live their lives driving one-way down the "stress lane" because of their total dependence on others. They create their own stress by having to manage so many other people who are doing their work for them. We're referring to constant dependence due to sheer laziness and lack of discipline.

The High Cost of Dependence

Karen writes: Living in San Diego has opened my eyes to the reality of those who choose to be dependent on others. Fact is stranger than fiction. Harris mentioned people in Los Angeles opting to hit the car wash instead of washing their own cars. I couldn't agree more, but that's just the tip of the lazy iceberg. What follows is a true story, but even though I experienced it myself I still can't believe it. This is what happens when parents unknowingly teach their kids to be dependent by giving them absolutely everything they want without requiring the kids to put forth anything near an equivalent effort for their end rewards. Even worse, it describes many of today's young families.

A Blessing or a Curse?

Say you're 21 and your father has money. Would you rather earn your own way or take advantage of the handout and have to cater to his every demand for the rest of your life as a result of your poor choice? This man chose the road to quick money over self-reliance. It was OK to get his girlfriend pregnant at 17 and have two kids by age 21 because his Dad had money. He was able to buy a brand new house, drive brand new cars of their choice and add endless upgrades to "their" house, since it's not "their" money.

Are they happy? Not even close. The exact opposite is true. Looking for ways to spend Dad's money is really taking its toll on the entire family! There's mention of depression and stress in every conversation. The wife has never worked and doesn't aspire to. Her kids are in daycare and full-time preschool so she doesn't have to raise them. Managing the maid service, grocery delivery and lawn maintenance people is a full-time job for her. After I had gotten up early to do my grocery shopping, some house cleaning and washed my car with my daughter we asked if they would like to walk to the park with us to play. She was so upset because she couldn't leave since the maids were cleaning inside and she had to wait for her groceries to be delivered. So I took the kids to the park and we played and had a good time. There she stood; looking frazzled while doing absolutely nothing.

They refuse to walk to school because the kids whine the whole way, so they drive. We live in a walking community with the school at its center for the expressed purpose of all residents being within walking distance. We walk there in 10 minutes and arrive before they do since it takes them longer to find a parking space. They are all overweight but don't understand why. The kids are having trouble in school. The wife is always on a quest to find people to take care of the kids for her and she's not shy about it. I would be depressed too if I had no purpose in life. I find it ironic that she is one who always comments that we have "the perfect life". No one's life is perfect. But comparatively, yes, I'd choose years of hard work, commitment, sacrifice and discipline over their empty life any day of the week.

> "The work of the individual still remains the sport that moves mankind ahead even more than teamwork."

Igor Sikorsky

Your Current Routine

> **"I wish I could stand on a busy corner, hat in hand, and beg people to throw me all their wasted hours."**
> *Bernard Berenson*

<u>You need to be on top of your days rather than your days being on top of you</u>. If you do what you've always done, you'll settle for mediocrity and struggle to get ahead. Is it enough or can you do better? Tell yourself that you need to stop the whining that you never have enough time to complete everything. We're sure you hear the same complaints from your friends, colleagues, and family. If you want to start making efficient use of your time then you must <u>change</u> your current routine.

In order to effectively prioritize your life and take full advantage of its magnificent powers you'll need to write down your current routine. Every day, hour, and minute of the month needs to be documented. The most significant wastes of time are in sleeping more than necessary, watching excessive television and commute time. The examples are based on the average of 6 hours of sleep a night. Find the minimum amount of sleep you need and adjust according to what works best for you. The same common sense should be exercised in the variables of your TV viewing and commute time.

Table 2.3 below is an example of the current 24-hour routine of a
Single Person:

Table 2.3: Current routine - single person

Daily Task	Time Started	Time Ended	Minutes Wasted
Wake up	6:00 a.m.	6:20 a.m. (after multiple snooze button bashings)	20
Shower & dress	6:20 a.m.	7:00 a.m.	0
Eat breakfast & read the paper	7:00 a.m.	7:30 a.m.	0
Drive to work	7:30 a.m.	8:30 a.m.	30 *(rush hour, avoid if at all possible)
Go out to lunch	12:00 p.m.	1:00 p.m.	30 (Going out *everyday* wastes time. Bring a bag lunch 4 days a week and treat yourself to eating out once a week
Drive home	5:30 p.m.	6:30 p.m.	30 *(rush hour, avoid if at all possible)
Unwind & watch TV	6:30 p.m.	7:30 p.m.	60 (if you're not exercising in the morning you need to do it here)
Prepare & eat dinner	7:30 p.m.	8:45 p.m.	0
Unwind/personal chores/TV	8:45 p.m.	11:00 p.m.	60 (assuming you're watching T.V. for one hour)
Sleep	11:00 p.m.	6:00 a.m.	0

Total # of Minutes Wasted = 230

Table 2.4 below is an example of the current 24-hour routine for a
Single Parent:

Table 2.4: Current routine - single parent

Daily Task	Time Started	Time Ended	Minutes Wasted
Wake up	6:00 a.m.	6:20 a.m. (after multiple snooze button bashings)	20
Have a cup of coffee	6:20 a.m.	6:35 a.m.	15
Shower & Dress	6:35 a.m.	7:05 a.m.	0
Prepare & eat breakfast for you & the kids & get the kids ready for school	7:05 a.m.	8:00 a.m.	0
Drive kids to daycare	8:00 a.m.	8:15 a.m.	0
Drive to work	8:15 a.m.	9:00 a.m.	0
Lunch break	12:00 p.m.	1:00 p.m.	30 (Going out *everyday* wastes time. Bring a bag lunch 4 days a week and treat yourself to eating out once a week
Drive to daycare/home	5:00 p.m.	6:00 p.m.	0
Prepare & eat dinner	6:00 p.m.	7:30 p.m.	0
Do homework with kids & prepare them for bed	7:30 p.m.	9:00 p.m.	0
Unwind/personal chores/TV	9:00 p.m.	11:00 p.m.	60 (assuming you're watching T.V for 1 hour)
Sleep	11:00 p.m.	6:00 p.m.	0

Total # of Minutes Wasted = 125

*Table 2.5 below is an example of a typical **weekend** routine for a*
Single Person:

Table 2.5: Current weekend routine - single person

Daily Task	Time Started	Time Ended	Minutes Wasted
Wake up	9:00 a.m.	9:30 a.m. (after multiple snooze button bashings)	30
Have Breakfast & read the paper	8:00 a.m.	9:00 a.m.	30 (If reading the paper is important to you then why not read it while you're on a stationery bike at home or at the gym).
Shower & dress	9:00 a.m.	10:00 a.m.	30
Do errands or household chores	10:00 a.m.	12:00 p.m.	0
Lunch	12:00 p.m.	12:30 p.m.	0
Watch TV	12:30 p.m.	5:00 p.m.	270 (There's more to do in life than watch T.V.)
Prepare & eat dinner	5:00 p.m.	6:15 p.m.	0
Shower & dress, prepare for a night out	6:15 p.m.	7:15 p.m.	0
Leisure time	7:15 p.m.	12:00 a.m.	0
Sleep	12:30 a.m.	9:00 a.m.	90 (7 hours of sleep is sufficient even on the weekend)
Total # of Minutes Wasted = 450			

Table 2.6 below is an example of the current 24-hour routine for a
Married Person _(without children):_

Table 2.6: Current routine - married person (without children)

Daily Task	Time Started	Time Ended	Minutes Wasted
Wake up	5:00 a.m.	5:30 a.m. (after multiple snooze button bashings)	30
Have Breakfast & read the paper	5:30 a.m.	6:30 a.m.	30 (If reading the paper is important to you then why not read it while you're on a stationery bike at home or at the gym).
Shower & dress	6:30 a.m.	7:15 a.m.	0
Drive to work	7:15 a.m.	8:00 a.m.	15 (rush hour commute)
Go out to lunch	12:00 p.m.	1:30 p.m.	60
Drive home	5:30 p.m.	6:15 p.m.	15 (rush hour commute)
Unwind & watch TV	6:15 p.m.	7:30 p.m.	60 (If you need to unwind 15 minutes is sufficient)
Prepare & eat dinner	7:30 p.m.	8:30 p.m.	0
Personal (paperwork, internet, etc.)	8:30 p.m.	10:00 p.m.	0
Sleep	10:00 p.m.	5:00 a.m.	0

Total # of Minutes Wasted = 210

*Table 2.7 below is an example of the current 24-hour **weekend** routine for a **Married Person (without children):***

Table 2.7: Current weekend routine - married person (without children)

Daily Task	Time Started	Time Ended	Minutes Wasted
Wake up	8:00 a.m.	8:30 a.m. (after multiple snooze button bashings)	30
Have Breakfast & read the paper	8:30 a.m.	10:00 a.m.	60 (If reading the paper is important to you then why not read it while you're on a stationery bike at home or at the gym).
Shower & dress	10:00 a.m.	10:45 a.m.	15
Do errands or household chores	10:45 a.m.	5:00 p.m.	0
Prepare & eat dinner	5:00 p.m.	6:30 p.m.	0
Go to a movie	6:30 p.m.	9:30 p.m.	0
Personal time with spouse	9:30 p.m.	11:00 p.m.	0
Sleep	11:00 p.m. (Saturday night)	8:00 a.m. (Sunday morning)	120 (7 hours of sleep is sufficient even on the weekend).
Total # of Minutes Wasted = 225			

Table 2.8 below is an example of the current 24-hour routine for a
Married Couple (with children):

Table 2.8: Current routine - married couple (with children)

Daily Task	Time Started	Time Ended	Minutes Wasted
Wake up	5:30 a.m.	5:45 a.m. (after multiple snooze button bashings)	15
Drink coffee & read the paper	5:45 a.m.	6:15 a.m.	30 (read the paper or watch the news while you're exercising on a tread mill or stationery bike)
Shower & dress	6:15 a.m.	6:45 a.m.	0
Get kids ready for school and have a light breakfast	6:45 a.m.	7:30 a.m.	0
Drive to daycare/work	7:30 a.m.	8:30 a.m.	0
Go out to lunch	12:00 p.m.	1:00 p.m.	30 (30 minute lunch breaks are sufficient you should only go out once a week if need be)
Drive to daycare/home	5:00 p.m.	6:00 p.m.	0
Do homework with kids	6:00 p.m.	6:45 p.m.	0
Prepare & eat dinner	6:45 p.m.	7:45 p.m.	0
Watch TV	7:45 p.m.	9:00 p.m.	0
Put kids to bed	9:00 p.m.	9:30 p.m.	0
Watch TV again	9:30 p.m.	11:00 p.m.	90 (There are better things to do than watch T.V.)
Sleep	11:00 p.m.	5:30 a.m.	0

Total # of Minutes Wasted = 165

*Table 2.9 below is an example of the current 24-hour **weekend** routine for a **Married Person (with children):***

Table 2.9: Current weekend routine – Married Person (with children)

Daily Task	Time Started	Time Ended	Minutes Wasted
Wake up	6:30 a.m.	6:45 a.m. (after multiple snooze button bashings)	15
Have breakfast, read the paper, and maybe have pancakes with the kids.	6:45 a.m.	8:00 a.m.	0
Shower & dress (entire family)	8:00 a.m.	9:00 a.m.	0
Play with the kids or take them on an outing.	9:00 a.m.	4:00 p.m.	0
Prepare and eat dinner	4:00 p.m.	5:30 p.m.	0
Watch TV	5:30 p.m.	11:00 p.m.	210 (2 hours of T.V. is more than enough)
Sleep	11:00 p.m. (Saturday night)	6:30 a.m. (Sunday morning)	30 (7 hours is sufficient)

Total # of Minutes Wasted = 255

Synopsis

It looks to us like there's room for improvement. Don't tell us you don't have time – PLEASE. When establishing your goals and priorities you need to take a very hard look at your current routine. Don't establish goals unless you seriously look at every minute and adjust accordingly. The tables below show our recommendations for improving your daily routine. It will provide you with the required adjustments to complete some of your newly established goals.

Recommended Routine

Table 2.10 below is an example of a disciplined **Single Person's** *recommended routine for a 24-hour period:*

Table 2.10: Recommended routine – single person

Daily Task	Time Started	Time Ended	Comments
Wake up	4:00 a.m.	4:00 a.m.	It may take a few weeks to adjust your body to the new early morning routine.
Wash face, brush teeth, go to the bathroom	4:00 a.m.	4:15 a.m.	
Have a <u>small</u> snack	4:15 a.m.	4:25 a.m.	
Dress for gym	4:25 a.m.	4:30 a.m.	
Drive to gym	4:30 a.m.	4:45 a.m.	
Exercise	4:50 a.m.	6:15 a.m.	The benefits of working out early are enormous: ➢ The gym is Less crowded ➢ More of the serious crowd- not a social scene ➢ Avoid crowded facility in the evening ➢ Your internal gears are already in motion. You don't have to sit around drinking coffee ➢ Your goal of consistently exercising will be achieved
Drive home	6:15 a.m.	6:30 a.m.	If it's possible to shower and shave at the gym you would save a few more minutes
Shower & shave	6:30 a.m.	7:00 a.m.	
Drive to work	7:00 a.m.	7:30 a.m.	Bypass peak traffic hour
Drive home	4:00 p.m.	4:30 p.m.	Bypass peak traffic hour
Prepare & eat dinner & cleanup	4:30 p.m.	6:00 p.m.	
Free time to work on your goals, read, etc.	6:00 p.m.	10:00 p.m.	
Sleep	10:00 p.m.	4:00 a.m.	6-7 hours of sleep is sufficient if you eat properly and consistently exercise

Minutes Wasted = 0

*Table 2.11 below is an example of a disciplined **Single Parent's** recommended routine for a 24-hour period.*

Table 2.11: Recommended routine – single person

Daily Task	Time Started	Time Ended	Comments
Wake up	4:00 a.m.	4:00 a.m.	
Wash face, brush teeth, go to the bathroom	4:00 a.m.	4:15 a.m.	
Have a small snack	4:15 a.m.	4:25 a.m.	
Prepare clothes and perhaps tidy up	4:25 a.m.	4:35 a.m.	
Prepare breakfast and lunches/clothes for you/kids	4:35 a.m.	5:00 a.m.	
Cardiovascular exercise for 30 minutes (hopefully you have a stationery bike or treadmill at home)	5:00 a.m.	5:30 a.m.	If you don't have a stationery bike or some other exercise machine then you need to exercise at lunch time or right after work before you pick up the kids from daycare
Take shower & dress	5:30 a.m.	6:00 a.m.	
Wake up kids & dress them. Everyone eats breakfast - then get kids ready for school	6:00 a.m.	7:00 a.m.	
Drive kids to daycare	7:00 a.m.	7:30 a.m.	
Drive to work	7:30 a.m.	8:30 a.m.	
Lunch break	12:00 p.m.	1:00 p.m.	
Drive to daycare/home	5:00 p.m.	6:00 p.m.	
Prepare & eat dinner	6:00 p.m.	7:00 p.m.	
Do homework with kids & prepare them for bed	7:00 p.m.	8:30 p.m.	
Unwind/cleanup/relax	8:30 p.m.	9:30 p.m.	
Sleep	9:30 p.m.	4:00 a.m.	6-7 hours of sleep is sufficient if you eat properly and consistently exercise

Minutes Wasted = 0

Table 2.12 below is an example of a disciplined **Single Person's** *recommended* **weekend** *routine for a 24-hour period:*

Table 2.12: Recommended weekend routine – single person

Daily Task	Time started	Time Ended	Comments
Wake up	5:00 a.m.	5:00 a.m.	Maintain the early morning exercise routine – you can treat yourself by sleeping in till 5 a.m. on the weekend – (if you need to) – otherwise continue to get up at 4am. If you go out on Friday night then you can sleep in a few hours later.
Wash face, brush teeth, go to the bathroom	5:00 a.m.	5:15 a.m.	
Have a small snack perhaps juice, ½ bagel, yogurt, banana or a combination	5:15 a.m.	5:25 a.m.	
Prepare clothes, tidy up, check email, etc.	5:25 a.m.	5:40 a.m.	To give yourself ample time to digest your food
Dress and drive to health club	5:40 a.m.	6:00 a.m.	
Exercise	6:00 a.m.	7:30 a.m.	
Shower & dress	7:30 a.m.	8:00 a.m.	
Do some errands, household chores, catch up on work, go have some fun, etc.	8:00 a.m.		From 8am on you have the rest of the day/evening to do whatever you heart desires.
Minutes Wasted = 0			

Table 2.13 below is an example of the recommended 24-hour routine for a disciplined **Married Person (without children):**

Table 2.13: Recommended routine – married person (without children

Daily Task	Time Started	Time Ended	Comments
Wake up	4:00 a.m.	4:00 a.m.	
Wash face, brush teeth, go to the bathroom	4:00 a.m.	4:15 a.m.	
Have a cup of juice and perhaps a small snack (½ bagel, yogurt, banana or a combination)	4:15 a.m.	4:30 a.m.	
Dress for the gym & perhaps take care of some personal chores.	4:30 a.m.	4:45 a.m.	To help you digest the small snack and save time when you get back from the gym. Your goal is to beat peak traffic hours.
Dress and drive to health club	4:45 a.m.	5:05 a.m.	
Exercise	5:10 a.m.	6:15 a.m.	
Drive home	6:15 a.m.	6:30 a.m.	
Shower & dress	6:30 a.m.	7:00 a.m.	If you can shower and dress at the gym you can save an additional 15 minutes (minimum).
Drive to work	7:00 a.m.	7:30 a.m.	
Work	7:30 a.m.	4:30 p.m.	
Drive home	4:30 p.m.	5:00 p.m.	
Prepare & eat dinner	5:00 p.m.	6:00 p.m.	
Clean up	6:00 p.m.	6:15 p.m.	
Read, personal time with spouse, computer time, etc.	6:15 p.m.	10:00 p.m.	
Sleep	10:00 p.m.	4:00 a.m.	6-7 hours of sleep is sufficient if you eat properly and consistently exercise

Minutes Wasted = 0

Table 2.14 below is an example of a disciplined **Married Person's (without children)** recommended **weekend** routine in a 24-hour period:

Table 2.14: Recommended weekend routine – married person without children

Daily Task	Time Started	Time Ended	Comments
Wake up	5:00 a.m. (Saturday morning)	5:00 a.m.	
Wash face, brush teeth, go to the bathroom	5:00 a.m.	5:15 a.m.	
Have a cup of juice and perhaps a small snack (1/2 bagel or banana or yogurt)	5:15 a.m.	5:30 a.m.	
Dress for the gym, & perhaps tidy up	5:30 a.m.	5:45 a.m.	To help you digest the small snack and save time when you get back from the gym. Your goal is to beat peak traffic hours
Drive to the health club and prepare to exercise	5:45 a.m.	6:05 a.m.	
Exercise	6:05 a.m.	7:15 a.m.	
Shower & dress	7:15 a.m.	7:45 a.m.	
Drive home	7:45 a.m.	8:00 a.m.	
Prepare & eat breakfast	8:00 a.m.	9:00 a.m.	
The rest of the day is yours to catch up on work, run errands, etc.	9:00 a.m.	5:00 p.m.	
Prepare to go out	5:00 p.m.	5:45 p.m.	
Go out to dinner and a night on the town	5:45 p.m.	12:00 a.m. (Sunday)	
Sleep	12:30 a.m. (Sunday)	6:30 a.m. (Sunday)	

Minutes Wasted = 0

*Table 2.15 below is an example of the recommended 24-hour routine for a disciplined **Married Couple (with children):***

Table 2.15: Recommended routine – married couple with children

Daily Task	Time Started	Time Ended	Comments
Husband <u>or</u> wife wakes up	4:00 a.m.	4:00 a.m.	
Wash face, brush teeth, go to the bathroom	4:00 a.m.	4:15 a.m.	
Have a cup of juice and perhaps a small snack (1/2 bagel or banana or yogurt	4:15 a.m.	4:30 a.m.	
Dress for the gym, & perhaps tidy up	4:30 a.m.	4:45 a.m.	To help you digest the small snack and save time when you get back from the gym. Your goal is to beat peak traffic hours
Husband <u>or</u> wife drives to the gym and begins exercising	4:45 a.m.	6:00 a.m.	
Husband or wife returns from gym and takes shower & dresses	6:00 a.m.	6:30 a.m.	
During this time spouse would get kids ready for school & serve breakfast	6:30 a.m.	7:30 a.m.	
Mom or dad drop kids off at school and drives to work	7:30 a.m.	8:30 a.m.	
Work	8:30 a.m.	5:30 p.m.	
Husband or wife would pickup kids from school, help with homework & prepare dinner while the other spouse goes to the gym	5:30 p.m.	7:00 p.m.	
Family eats dinner together	7:00 p.m.	7:30 p.m.	
Cleanup and get kids ready for bed	7:30 p.m.	8:15 p.m.	
Family time	8:15 p.m.	9:00 p.m.	
Bedtime for kids	9:00 p.m.	6:00 a.m.	
Personal time for husband & wife	9:00 p.m.	10:00 p.m.	
Sleep	10:00 p.m.	4:00 a.m.	

Minutes Wasted = 0

Table 2.16 below is an example of a disciplined **Married Person's (with children)** recommended **weekend** routine in a 24-hour period:

Table 2.16: Recommended weekend routine – married person with children

Daily Task	Time started	Time Ended	Comments
Wake up	4:00 a.m.	4:00 a.m.	If you want to spend quality time with your family and put everything you've got into your exercise routine then continue to wake up early. You don't want to short-change them
Brush teeth, wash face and go to the bathroom	4:00 a.m.	4:15 a.m.	
Have a cup of juice and perhaps have a small snack (1/2 bagel or piece of fruit or a yogurt)	4:15 a.m.	4:30 a.m.	
Dress for the gym & perhaps tidy up	4:30 a.m.	4:45 a.m.	To help you digest the small snack and save time when you get back from the gym. Your goal is to beat peak traffic hours
Drive to the health club and prepare to exercise	4:45 a.m.	5:05 a.m.	
Exercise	5:05 a.m.	6:15 a.m.	
Shower & drive back home	6:15 a.m.	7:00 a.m.	Take a shower at the gym
Prepare and eat breakfast with the family	7:00 a.m.	8:00 a.m.	
Family outing	8:00 a.m.	4:00 p.m.	
Come home, prepare dinner, and eat with the family	4:00 p.m.	6:00 p.m.	
Family time for games, movie, or TV	6:00 p.m.	8:45 p.m.	
Put kids to bed.	8:45 p.m.	9:00 p.m.	
Personal time with spouse	9:00 p.m.	10:00 p.m.	
Sleep	10:00 p.m.	4:00 a.m.	

Minutes Wasted = 0

Synopsis

The way to kill time profitably is to work it to death.

"Every morning you are handed 24 golden hours.
They are one of the few things in this world that
you get free of charge. If you had all the money
in the world, you couldn't buy an extra hour.
What will you do with this priceless treasure?"
Source Unknown

If you were to associate a price tag to every minute you've wasted you would
be one rich individual. So once again, don't tell us you don't have the time!

Structure

"One today is worth two tomorrows."
Franklin

We know exactly what you're going to say. "It's bad enough that I need to have
a structured routine at work. From the time I get in the car, subway, bus, etc.,
until the time I get home. Why would I want structure 24 hours a day?
Wouldn't a managed lifestyle stress me out more than I already am?" Now let
us ask you a question. Wouldn't you want to have more time to relax, to play
with your kids or even more time to do nothing? With a structured lifestyle you
will gain back some of those precious minutes you currently throw away every
day on nonsense. Those minutes will add up to hours by weeks end. Structure
will make your life easier to manage. Its not only children who thrive in a
structured environment, adults function best with one also.

As depicted in tables 2.3 – 2.9 you waste an average of 4 hours each day. Of
those 2 hours why not document (in your new routine- see table 2.17) two
hours of personal time and/or relaxation and two hours of productive time?
It's that simple. You can <u>easily</u> have the balanced lifestyle you've been seeking.
The charts below are the tools that will help you take control.

Below are your own personal charts for tracking your Current Routine. Make a few copies of this as well as the PRIME Routine chart (Table 2.18). This will allow you to adjust accordingly to your changing routine. Additional rows are provided for you to customize as necessary. Experiment with every aspect of your Daily Tasks until you find the level of balance that makes the very best use of your time every day.

My Current Routine

Table 2.17: My current routine

Daily Task	Time Started	Time Ended	Minutes Wasted
Wake up			
Wash face, brush teeth, go to the bathroom			
Have a small snack			
Prepare breakfast			
Exercise			
Shower & dress			
Drive to work			
Lunch break			
Drive home			
Prepare and eat dinner			
Unwind, clean up, relax			
Sleep			

Once you have it down on paper you can now begin to focus on those areas where minutes are being wasted. This is where flexibility and creativity come into play. We've provided you with some ideas for manipulating your time. Or as we like to call it - getting you PRIMED. See the Creative Time Savers section for guidance. The ways in which you can utilize time is endless, search them out and challenge yourself to find them.

Make Your Routine Public Knowledge

Sit down and figure out exactly what you need to do everyday and make it routine. Don't waste the gift of extra time that you've worked so hard to achieve. Then you can PRIME it all and inform everyone what your schedule is. This is extremely important because there are always people who think your time is somehow less important then theirs. They will take as much of your time as you allow them to take. Don't allow this vicious cycle to ever begin. Schedule time for what is important to you.

Suggestions for Making the Leap to the PRIME of Your Life

The definition of the word PRIME in the dictionary contains the following: *"To make ready; prepare. To prepare someone or something for future action or operation. To prepare with information; coach. To encourage the growth of something. First in excellence, quality or value. The period or phase of ideal or peak condition."*

Charting your routine should be viewed as a critical stepping-stone that will take you to the next level. Make every effort to utilize your charts. This point can't be stressed enough. Once you've got your PRIME routine down to a science, then you won't need to rely on your charts anymore. Before you know it, you'll be PRIMED and ready to take on dreams that you thought you never had time for.

Your PRIME routine is now firmly imbedded in your mind and operating on autopilot. View yourself as the computer and the charts as computer programs. The more effective and detailed your charts are, the more efficient you will be. The old "garbage in/garbage out" metaphor certainly applies here.

Creative Time Savers

Here are some ideas that can help you tweak your Daily Tasks to get you operating in PRIME time.

Wake Up: Seems pretty straight forward, doesn't it? If you didn't need to get up when your alarm went off, then why did you set it at that time to begin with? Maybe instead of giving your clock a good whack you should smack yourself for not having the discipline to get up the first time it went off! We're sure the inventor of the snooze button had good intentions. It's proof positive that if you give someone an excuse to be lazy they will take full advantage of it.

Solution: Buy a clock that doesn't have a snooze button or simply move your clock away from the bed so you have to get up to turn it off. Maybe putting it in the bathroom will encourage you to stay there and get on with your morning. Get a clock radio/CD player so you can wake up to your favorite music if that helps get you moving.

Go to the Bathroom: We think its safe to say, you can handle the porcelain bowl on your own terms. But you really should "aim to please" here, because if you don't, you'll have to spend more time cleaning up after yourself later. Trust us on this one...everyone has better things to do with their time than clean the toilet!

A true classic time saver enjoyed by men everywhere is reading in the bathroom. We have to give men credit for this one. Sometimes it's more about stealing a minute of peace and privacy than "multitasking". With reading material in hand it's symbolism at its best. It sends a clear message: Take notice that this man is on a mission---he's got business, it's going to take a while---and he shouldn't be bothered--- anyone who dares to enter his temporary work space will suffer the consequences. It's pure genius! Sure it's a bit outdated, but illustrates that even back when the world moved much slower, undisturbed time was still cherished.

Shower: If getting into a cold shower wakes you up, then go for it. Do you prefer a warm shower? While waiting for it to warm up do something else.

Solution: Brush and/or floss your teeth. Some electric toothbrushes work on a 2-minute timer. It forces you to practice good dental hygiene that will hopefully save you time in the dentist office later. Halfway through brushing your teeth you can get the shower going so it's ready when you are. Make the bed, do some stretches or whatever little task you can squeeze in that will keep you moving.

Dress: Having your clothes ready the night before is always best. If you're not a "morning person" you might waste time deciding on something, find out something wasn't washed or just feel rushed. It's just one less thing to deal with first thing in the morning.

Breakfast: Prior planning is important again. Make sure everyone has something healthy, quick, and easy to prepare. You can eat while you read the newspaper or catch the morning news and weather report. This is not optional; please give your body something decent to get your day off to a good start.

Drive to work: We have to get to work and so we face the dreaded commute. Most jobs don't allow flexibility in this area due to the nature of the job. If this is the case and you're hitting the worst part of rush hour, it's definitely worth some experimentation. Take a look at how much time you spend commuting and decide the best way to play it.

> **Solution:** You won't know if you can get those hours back if you don't try. It may call for some creative planning strategies, especially where daycare is concerned, but look into it. If it gets back an hour or more in your day to be with your kids or to further your career, then everyone wins. Try coming to work earlier than normal. Do the math and figure out what the optimum time is. If you don't find any options, then make the best of it. Listen to books on tape to learn something new.
>
> If you are fortunate enough to create some flexibility with your job then you may be able to create options here. It never hurts to ask. Talk to your employer about the possibility of coming in earlier if you know you are more productive in the morning hours. Come in after rush hour and leave later if that suits you better. You are not only being more productive for the company by working when you're at your best, but you are exchanging that commute time for personal

time. Even if only one spouse is able to strike this deal, the entire family will benefit. The parent who leaves earlier will be able to pick up the kids and spend that time with them as opposed to sitting in traffic. They can get a jump on homework and dinner so everyone has more time to be together later.

Prepare and Eat Dinner: If you want to eat well and do it in minimum time there are a few things you can do to keep your weeknights easy. The trend of cooking meals once a month is becoming popular so the freezer is full of individual meals ready to heat and serve. If you're not into spending one weekend a month on a cooking marathon there are other options. Consider cooking a few meals on the weekend, freeze them if necessary and eat those leftovers on weekdays. You will only have to spend mere minutes making salads or vegetables to go with that main course. It beats fast food any day of the week and it blows 30 minutes off our Recommended Routine chart! A couple nights you can cook something new to keep things interesting, but it should always be kept quick and simple. The best of both worlds is to cook with your spouse and/or family to share the task as well as spend time together. This is a classic example of turning a simple daily task into lifelong memories as well as doing it in minimum time. It's a PRIME example, no doubt.

Watch TV: Did you notice we're not big TV watchers? Sure, we have our favorites and we watch them. But if your TV goes on when you walk in the door and stays on until you go to bed…then we suggest you shut off your TV and try reading this in peace and quiet. OK, use the mute button if you're not ready to go cold turkey, but please read on.

> **Solution:** Program the VCR to record ONLY your favorite shows. Spend time with your family each evening, read, listen to music, walk the dog, do essential chores and when you have absolutely nothing to do; then go ahead and pop in your recorded shows. Fast forward through the mind-numbing commercials and by the way, isn't technology wonderful when you are actually using it to enhance your life? Recapture all those hours you previously wasted.

> We've known people who simply moved their televisions out of their family rooms and into an area that wasn't centrally located. Still others did the unthinkable and put theirs in the attic for a while to see how different their lives would be without it. To this day they are relishing in the fact that they are getting their news from the radio, the Internet and newspaper. As an added bonus, their children pick up books on a regular basis, just for the opportunity to learn something new. Just

because we're fortunate enough to live in such a technologically advanced world doesn't mean we should let it take over our lives. It should be used to enhance your life, not detract from the truly important things.

If you are home because you are sick, with a new baby, or whatever do yourself a favor and look elsewhere for entertainment. We really hope you don't allow yourself to be sucked into the timeless hell that is daytime TV. If it helps, feel free to apply the rule we use in our house. If it's not educational or funny, then it's not worth watching.

If your TV has a timer button, use it. Set it so your kids have limits and know when their TV time is up. It seems as the year's pass we are finding more adult subjects being shown at times when kids would normally be watching. Be it early morning or after school, the advertising alone can be very disturbing for children, not to mention the regular programs.

And if you're breaking out in a sweat after reading the "attic" story, maybe you should consider using the timer on yourself.

Movies: We think the high school and college crowd are the target audiences who frequent movie theatres with any regularity. It's perfect for those times when you just have to get out and want to do something entertaining. Then you probably don't mind standing in lines waiting to buy tickets because you're just hanging out with friends anyway. Even if the flick is a stinker you'll probably pick up some great jokes to use whenever the opportunity presents itself, so it's not a total loss.

Once you have a family your priorities change and suddenly the appeal of surround sound and chewing gum on the bottom of your shoes doesn't do it for you anymore. You'll utilize one or all of the other options available to avoid the inevitable disappointment of allowing the entire movie theater routine to occupy such a huge block of your time.

> **Solution:** If we didn't know so many people who go to movies and complain about the experience we wouldn't bother writing this. Hit a matinee when there aren't lines to contend with and save yourself a few bucks. Even at its best, we still have issues with people who see movie theaters as their own personal junk food buffets. We're always compelled to check the expiration date on our CPR card to be sure we're not up for a refresher course just in case our skills are required before the credits roll. We do a mental refresher regardless.

If you prefer watching movies rather than listening to the sound of 200 people snarfing down popcorn, then you probably have cable, satellite or whatever brings the flicks directly to you. We frequent our local movie rental establishment because we like to get them only when we make the time and only after several friends have recommended them. Two hours is just too long to waste on a bad movie when there are so many good ones to see.

There are even DVD's available for rent on the Internet. A website advertises that you receive and return them in the mail, rent as many as you like and keep them as long as you want. Sounds like it's too good to be true. We can't recommend them because we haven't tried them. We don't want to feel obligated to spend our time watching movies every month. Do the research if you like this option.

Internet Time: Talk about your time vacuum. Ever notice how many "time saving" gadgets there are on the market? You'd think time management was a problem in our society or something! It seems the more gizmos we have, the less time we have and more stress comes along with them.

Karen writes: Watch your Internet time carefully. I was on an Internet list for about 6 months or so. I loved it because it was for parents whose kids were born in my daughter's birth month. We always had a lot to share and discuss. I just had to abandon it because although I made some very cool friends that way, it just sucked away hours of my evening time and my inbox was flooded with a minimum of 50 new emails everyday from the list. Although I was learning and able to help others at the same time I couldn't afford to give that much time.

Set a timer and get off the computer when it goes off. This is really the best way to manage it. It also goes a long way towards using timers on your kids without catching a lot of flak. They will follow your lead and recognize that moderation is important.

Once you've successfully exchanged Minutes Wasted for whatever is more important in your life, then you are ready to finalize using your PRIME routine chart.

Table 2.18 below is your own personal chart for your new PRIME routine.

My PRIME Routine

Table 2.18: My PRIME routine

Daily Task	Time Started	Time Ended	Minutes Wasted
Wake up			
Wash face, brush teeth, go to the bathroom			
Have a small snack			
Prepare breakfast			
Exercise			
Shower & dress			
Drive to work			
Lunch break			
Drive home			
Prepare and eat dinner			
Unwind, clean up, relax			
Sleep			

You now have the tools in place to achieve discipline in its purest form. You've set goals, prioritized in order to attain them and are making the changes in your lifestyle to support those goals. You are working automatically in PRIME Time.

Tools Of The Trade

> "I never could have done what I have done without the habits of punctuality, order, and diligence, without the determination to concentrate myself on one subject at a time..."
> *Charles Dickens*

Karen writes: Your PRIME is in place to manage blocks of time in your daily schedule. Now we need to get a handle on all the "stuff of life" or the details that make your schedule seem so out of control. You know, those appointments, shopping, household chores, family events, time for your spouse and last but never least – time for yourself. This is what trips us women up because we are usually the ones doing this dance so this is critical for our sanity.

All this can be totally overwhelming but it doesn't have to be. If you want to see where all your time is going utilize a planner that works for you. I'm talking about finally documenting those days filled with mind numbing tasks that leave you feeling like you're inside a hamster ball going nonstop but there isn't much to show for all your efforts at the end of the day except exhaustion. This is not only important for you, but if you're the Commander In Chief of the house then your significant other will appreciate you so much more when they see what they're "missing" by working outside the home.

Choose Your Weapon

> "Much may be done in those little shreds and patches of time, which every day produces, and which most men throw away, but which nevertheless will make at the end of it no small deduction for the life of man."
> *Charles Caleb Colton*

Decide if you prefer writing things down to remember or if you remember appointments better by the day or date they are on. For writers, the tool of choice is the paper day planner. For those who think chronologically an electronic planner or Personal Digital Assistant (PDA) is your weapon of choice. Being able to track hours and especially minutes is what is important.

To use your weapon effectively you have to schedule <u>everything</u>. Not just your appointments but errands, laundry, bill paying and calls to make. Ask yourself how long each task takes and when is the best time to tackle it. Figuring out the time it takes to accomplish your tasks is one of the very first things you'll learn in any time management course. This will banish your endless to-do lists forever. Once you have each minute or hour of your day scheduled then you see exactly what each day has in store.

The Gift of Time

> "Time has a wonderful way of weeding out the trivial."
> *Howard Aiken*

Karen writes: I got my husband a PDA for Christmas – well, that was the original plan anyway. When I started playing with it I realized how much easier it would be to maintain my own schedule than my current paper planner. I had to have it! We got him another one that had a few more bells and whistles to satisfy the boy gene. That also turned out to be a good thing since we can synchronize them to download each other's schedule or whatever is important to be passed on so we're not forgetting important things that require both of us to be present. I use mine to schedule my minutes, but he uses his to schedule appointments and to keep up with me. This electronic planner has changed my life so dramatically that I truly feel as if I have been given the gift of more time for <u>everything</u>. Once you can see that your time is tangible you suddenly find it so much easier to delegate to other family members and say no to things you clearly don't have time for.

3. YOUR LIFE, INC.

> "Knowing is not enough;
> We must apply.
> Willing is not enough;
> We must do.
> *Goethe*

As we mentioned earlier acquiring discipline is so much more than writing down your goals and priorities, now it's time for action. Goethe couldn't have said it any better – it's time to "apply" and "do".

Why wouldn't you? What are you waiting for? The clock of life is ticking - YOUR CLOCK. You have your PRIME, you know how to train the mind, you can't use those lame excuses anymore. So if you're not going to change your life for the better then take responsibility for it because you have no one else to blame but yourself.

> "Take your life into your own hands and what
> happens? A terrible thing; no one to blame."
> *Erica Jong*

It's a lot of work but you know as well as we do that there are no short cuts to places worth going! It reminds me of what we are forced to do when we are faced with a tough decision. We think long and hard. Quick fixes rarely are sufficient unless you want a temporary solution. Anything that is of importance or that can have a significant impact on our lives is worth the additional time and effort required.

> "I was taught that the way of progress is neither
> swift nor easy."
> *Marie Curie*

Many of us dream or fantasize about being successful in life but dreaming about it is one thing and actually making it a reality is another. Walt Disney said, "If you can dream it, you can do it". These are words of encouragement from a man whose legacy surpassed his own dreams and became reality for future generations to enjoy. To actually fulfill some of those dreams and aspirations requires one thing - discipline. Without it you'll never be able to fulfill all of your dreams and aspirations.

In order to acquire discipline you will need to manage your life as if it were a business. Your livelihood and perhaps your family's livelihood depend on it. You've been saving up for and dreaming about this business most of your life. This is something you'll be taking on with passion. It's human nature to be passionate about what is ours and this is especially true of Your Life, Inc. It requires every ounce of mental and physical strength you can muster to be successful. It's not as daunting as it seems. This is what it takes to get your life focused and ultimately headed toward fulfilling your dreams. It's well worth it.

Starting and managing your own business is a 24/7 commitment. All start-ups require nothing less than a full-time effort. In the beginning there is no relaxation, no holidays and very few days off, if any. As with any business, it starts by building the foundation, i.e., business plan, financing, customer base, vendors, office space, etc. The same goes for your personal foundation, which will be built on discipline.

You control every aspect of the business. The power is within you to succeed. There is a great sense of freedom and satisfaction that business owners possess. In order to keep that freedom they must work that much harder to ensure success. Working hard for yourself is doing what you love more hours of the day. Working hard for someone else is just that and nothing more. Harris says, "The only partnership in this business is you against you (as discussed in my first book titled: *Discipline: Six Steps to Unleashing Your Hidden Potential* the section titled: *The Mirror*)." Hopefully you like yourself because you've only got yourself to blame if this "partnership" fizzles. If you don't like what you see in the mirror, your quest for discipline will change that. You already know discipline is important, otherwise you wouldn't be reading this.

> "Your talent is God's gift to you. What you do
> with it is your gift back to God."
> Leo Buscaglia

If you want something that will alter your entire life and allow you to accomplish more than you ever thought possible, then you'll have to earn it the old fashioned way. Once you've acquired discipline, then you can take some time off to enjoy the fruits of your labor. However, this is ongoing and it normally takes years if its done right. If you are not among the privileged that were taught discipline as children, then you must learn it now. Don't let the duration bother you. You want a solid, reliable, experienced corporation that has earned the trust of its customers. This is simply one of those things that need time to develop. The time will fly by anyway because you won't be wasting it. Karen says, "My mom always used to say, 'Busy hands are happy hands!' That made her an easy target for many sarcastic adolescent jokes but she was right and we knew it."

The benefits package is incredible! It's very comprehensive and the bennies are realized as quickly as you work to earn them. The list is enormous, but one of the best perks is knowing at the end of each day that you've lived that day to the fullest.

To acquire discipline and accomplish more than ever your life has to be managed in the same manner. Personal and professional events and activities need to be prioritized as if your life was that business. Year after year there is so much more you want to accomplish but as the years go by you have significantly less time.

When you're managing Your Life, Inc. everything is prioritized with every minute of the day being accounted for. There are no excuses and you must <u>always</u> make things happen.

> **"Success or failure in business is caused more by the mental attitude even than by mental capacities."**
> *Sir Walter Scott*

Attitude is everything. Change is a good thing. You're expected to change everyday. Be dissatisfied. Change your life's goals. This is that extremely powerful moment when your discontent and aspirations crystallize. The decision is quick and final. Life is short, it's time to establish Your Life, Inc. and own it in all its entirety.

Use your positive attitude to push you forward. It's when we want something most passionately that we hardly notice the risks. This is where you want to be. Do not allow self-doubt to hold you back anymore. Your desire and will to change are much more powerful, so use them to your advantage.

Never Compare Yourself to Someone Else

"When you are content to be simply yourself and don't compare or compete, everybody will respect you."
Lao-Tzu

If you want to be successful in every facet of life never compare yourself to anyone else. People have a tendency to compare themselves to others. Normally it's people they aspire to be or look like i.e., movie stars, athletes, etc. Never spend the time or energy to be like someone else. It's OK to analyze or read about them but you need to stay within your own boundaries.

Once you've acquired discipline you'll be happy with yourself and you'll never compare yourself or aspire to be like anyone. You'll have the total package that contains all the attributes that come with discipline. Like it or not, you will become the one who others will want to emulate. Discipline is highly contagious.

Feel Good About Yourself

"Love yourself first and everything else falls into line. You really have to love yourself to get everything done in this world."
Lucille Ball

We never imagined we would put a quote from Lucille Ball in our book, but very few could have said it any better. To become successful you need to feel good about yourself. Always have a positive outlook on your life and your goals and priorities. In order to be successful in anything you take on you need to like yourself. You need to get to that point when you have confidence in yourself and the best way to do that is to follow your PRIME. Your PRIME will help you become successful. Once you start accomplishing a few goals and keeping your commitments how could you not start feeling good about yourself? You will finally be gaining control. Being in control of your time, your goals and your priorities is what will lead you to a fulfilling life.

Obstacles

"Obstacles don't have to Stop You. If you run Into a Wall, Don't turn around and Give Up. Figure out how to Climb It, Go Through It, or Work Around It."
Michael Jordan

Life is full of obstacles. It's no news flash. We are all painfully aware of them and they make themselves known to us on a daily basis. They come in all different types and they impact different areas (i.e., personal, financial, health, etc.). They're all difficult to deal with but they should never stop you. Regardless of the problem, you're on a mission and you have a plan (PRIME). Now it's time to focus.

Obstacles are those frightful things you see when you take your eyes off your goal.
Henry Ford

These obstacles could slow you down a bit but that's expected. Slow is one thing but hitting the wall and stopping is another.

"When you come to a roadblock, take a detour"
Mary Kay Ash

Temptations

Karen writes: These are sometimes the biggest obstacles we will face. If your health becomes a goal, then decadent foods or sweets can be one of your biggest temptations or obstacles to overcome. Being someone who loves to bake and enjoy dessert I butt heads with this one on a regular basis. I've learned that I love the process as much as the end result and its more about giving my time doing something for those I love but the final product is just an added bonus. But it can quickly become added weight too if it becomes a habit and you don't have a plan to control it. I'm speaking from experience. It doesn't surprise me that stressed spelled backwards is desserts. It's a way of pampering yourself when you feel you really deserve something that is very good and very bad simultaneously. You don't have to make anything yourself anymore. You can get it anytime, anywhere and that's why its such a lethal form of addiction to begin with – availability.

As a result, I don't bake nearly as much as I would like anymore because I know that means longer walks or increased treadmill time. But for those times when it's worth putting forth that extra effort to indulge then I have options. I eat smaller portions that are usually split with someone else or made that way on purpose. At least half of it either goes into a care package for someone else or on a plate to a neighbor's house. Make something very low calorie so it's not an issue. I can have my cake and eat it too, I just can't have it as frequently as I would like and I have to account for every bite so I don't sabotage my goal of good health.

Don't think you can go into a bakery and window shop. If you don't have ways to moderate your temptation then why are you torturing yourself? You simply shouldn't go there if you haven't considered how adversely those calories will affect your other goals. Steer clear of it if you know your willpower is low. Evasive action is very critical! I can usually window shop and the smell alone is enough to make me feel as if I just ate a bite and I can almost feel those pounds and that heavy feeling after eating it that makes you wonder why you didn't just keep going. Don't focus on how good it tastes, that is only temporary. The digestive process takes much longer and those hours which follow and the weight that comes later are what you need to consider before giving into that temptation. Mind games (see Chapter 6) to the rescue once again - use them!

The same rules apply to whatever your temptation might be. It might be gambling, shopping or any number of things, but your vices should all be treated the same way. Society plays on our weaknesses through advertising and they're very good at it because billions of dollars are put into their efforts. Don't allow yourself to get sucked in.

Las Vegas is called "Sin City" because a majority of the population is intrigued by the thought of it. Slick advertising that lures the weak into believing that you can check your morals at the door and it's OK, because "you're in Vegas" so anything goes! You can't go to sin city and not commit a sin, what kind of a spineless wimp are you anyway? You can spend your money on gambling, family entertainment, or at strip clubs. Seems there are more vices to indulge in than things that people with values can enjoy. It's not true, but that is where they make most of their money and they put lots of it back into advertising. You have so many options before you that it's overwhelming at first glance. Seems every casino on the strip has the "loosest slots" in town so how can you lose? You can't drive a mile without being bombarded with pictures of silicon enhanced, plastic surgeon manufactured showgirls. What will you do? If you're married and you think your spouse is "cool with the strip club thing" because everyone else is doing it then you better be prepared to deal with any "weakness" that your spouse may indulge in. We're sure you will be "cool with it" because you've got that whole give and take thing going on, right? If you know that making evasive maneuvers is what you'd expect your spouse to do, then you're expected to do the same. Would it bother or surprise men to see their wife or daughter up on a strip club stage? Guess it depends on the man.

Never allow temptations to sideline Your Life, Inc. Your health and happiness depend on your ability to achieve discipline in every aspect of your life.

Working Hard

> "Don't be afraid to give your best to what seemingly are small jobs. Every time you conquer one it makes you that much stronger. If you do the little jobs well, the big ones tend to take care of themselves."
> *Dale Carnegie*

Hard work is still one of the best tools you have to acquire discipline. Whether it's your job, your exercise routine, or personal life hard work will always be the key to success in every facet of life. But it's not only about working hard, it's working smart and that's where prime comes in. PRIME + hard work = discipline <u>and</u> a balanced life.

Continuously Challenge Yourself

> "What lies behind us and what lies before us are tiny matters, compared to what lies within us."
> *Ralph Waldo Emerson*

Harris writes: My first book focused on the relationship between you and yourself (The man in the mirror) where a person takes a hard look in the mirror and continually challenges him or herself, but stays within their boundaries. By acquiring discipline you get to know your mind and body as well as what it can and cannot handle. Many people get themselves in too deep. Do not set goals so far out of reach that failure will be imminent.

> "You must do the thing you think you cannot do."
> *Eleanor Roosevelt*

Without continuous challenge, you will not succeed! I frequently challenge myself; it is automatic, like brushing teeth. I feel like superman - mentally and physically prepared for anything. As I am busy fulfilling my chaotic travel schedule as well as the other commitments in my life, I can't help but feel that it's this "leaping tall buildings in a single bound" feeling that keeps me reaching for more.

Commitment

> "Until one is committed there is hesitancy, the chance to draw back, always ineffectiveness. Concerning all acts of initiative (and creation), there is one elementary truth, the ignorance of which kills countless ideas and splendid plans: that the moment one definitely commits oneself, the Providence moves too. All sorts of things occur to help one that would never otherwise

> have occurred. A whole stream of events issues
> from the decision, raising in one's favour all
> manner of unforeseen incidents and meetings
> and material assistance, which no man could
> have dreamt would have come his way."
> *W.H. Murray*

Commitment is the key to success with all endeavors. It cannot be half-hearted commitment for that is not commitment. It needs to be all out "do or die" commitment. Your mind and body have to want it and be completely behind it. The official definition of commitment is: Dedication to a long-term course of action, engagement, and involvement. The two key words are dedication and long-term. Once you commit to something to have to eat, breathe, and live with that commitment. Each one of your goals needs 100% commitment in order to be successful.

Having Fun

Is it possible to still have fun while you're trying to acquire discipline? Of course you can have fun, as long as you set aside time for it and it doesn't interfere with your other goals. Based on your timeline for acquiring discipline it's how much time you allot for fun. Fun can mean different things for different people. Perhaps for reader A it's going out once a week to drink and party their hearts out. For reader B it could mean a vacation every 3 months and for reader C it could mean sitting around every Sunday drinking a few beers and watching sporting events all day long. To each his own, but once you establish your goals and priorities you must stick to it. How much time did you allot for fun? It's a matter of what your priorities are. The best scenario is to love your occupation so you are able to have fun at work. That's what it means to have it all.

Being Unconventional

Karen writes: Its no mistake that this follows the section on having fun. For me doing things out of the ordinary is nothing more than a way to accomplish a goal and have fun while doing it. Often times the conventional solution is not the best one for me. This comes naturally when you begin to constantly challenge yourself to find better ways to meet your goals. What others think isn't important because I know what is important to me and that is what really matters. Sometimes those who lack confidence will not be unconventional because of their fear of what others think. That's a shame. If the great thinkers and inventors of our time cared what others thought about their ideas we'd still be living the dark ages. The times when we hit a brick wall and feel the frustration of tackling a problem is when we are most likely to call on our creativity to break down that wall for us and for all who follow. A solution cannot be found until the problem presents itself. Seize the opportunity to be unconventional.

As far back as I can remember I was doing things differently and in my own way. I was given dolls to play with as a child but I preferred doing things that challenged me as well as my imagination. At the age of 7 I was given the opportunity to choose a puppy of my own from a litter of our Norwegian Elkhounds and I immediately trained her to do what I loved to do. That meant she was very disciplined in all the conventional ways, but when the trainer is an unconventional puppy herself the result will always be something extraordinary. After grueling and frustrating training she was trained to love riding in my wagon, baby carriage and the wheel barrel. I had trained her too well in fact. If she was anywhere near anything that moved she would bolt out of nowhere and jump in, so getting her out became a challenge. I think the baby carriage was the accomplishment I cherished most. Pushing around a doll is normal. Pushing around my dog with her legs dangling through the leg holes for as long as I cared to was my idea of self-made fun. I accomplished many more goals than I had originally set out to and both of us were enjoying the ride. It didn't end there. I wrote a book of poems about training my puppy for my second grade class, complete with pictures so the conventional kids could see for themselves. Here it is 30 years later and I am still writing about the virtues of discipline. The impact it had on me then still feels as wonderful as it does in my life today. History repeating itself is a clear sign that my unconventional ways and discipline have everything to do with the person I am and always have been. My life has always been challenging, fun and exciting because I refuse to settle for anything less.

Another flashback of my unconventional attitude takes me back to fifth grade. I had just won the spelling bee and the winner of the other class and I were waiting to hear what we had won. I loved my teacher, Mrs. Blomquist, but you could've heard a pin drop when she happily announced to everyone that our prize was to come to her house for dinner with her husband and she would make us anything we wanted. Talk about your anti-prize! The only thing worse would've been to share this "prize" with a boy. We were both still reeling from the concept of our worlds colliding when we'd have to go to our teacher's house. She pressed us to share what we wanted for dinner right then and there. No pressure! The other girl, Jenny, shrugged her shoulders and told me she didn't care what we had. I said, "Lobster with butter, salad with Ranch dressing, baked potato with sour cream, pop to drink and whatever dessert you are best at making. Can you make us that? And does that sound good to you, Jenny?" Everyone was laughing, but that wasn't my intent. Living on a farm we ate beef in every form on a regular basis and this was my chance to have something that I had never experienced before and knew we couldn't afford. Almost everything on that menu was not found on our dinner table, except the potatoes, which would never leave, no matter how hard I prayed. Those were a staple for us, but the sour cream was a bonus. Yeah, I was pretty unconventional for 10 but I'm not afraid to ask for what I really want when I know I've earned it. We also got tickets to see Dorothy Hamill at the Ice Capades before we left that "Twilight Zone" dinner experience. For some odd reason that prize paled in comparison to my first stab at coloring outside the lines where opportunity is concerned.

Never be Satisfied

> Look at a day when you are supremely satisfied at the end. It's not a day when you lounge around doing nothing; it's when you've had everything to do, and you've done it.
> *Lord Acton*

The more you accomplish in a 24-hour period the more satisfied you'll be at the end of the day. The secret is to stay hungry and never be completely satisfied. The best thing you can do is to keep piling up those tasks as long as they're meaningful. The more tasks you have on your plate the hungrier you will be and complete satisfaction will be a figment of your imagination.

It's important not to become a workaholic in pursuit of your many accomplishments. No one lying on their deathbed regrets not having spent more time at work. The true measure of a person's success and happiness is their emotional, physical and psychological well-being. What we're saying is to never be satisfied with the level of happiness you've attained. There are always areas in our lives that need attention to keep the balance consistent. Being happy in all aspects of your life is the mother of all accomplishments. Don't settle. If you must, remember to always settle for more.

There's Always a Solution

> "When one door closes another door opens; but we so often look so long and so regretfully upon the closed door, that we do not see the ones which open for us."
> *Alexander Graham Bell*

Every problem has a solution. Sometimes it's not in front of you and it might not always be straightforward but there is a solution out there. Be persistent and stay determined. If you want something bad enough, and you make it a goal, you will eventually get it. Patience and perseverance are extremely powerful in the hands of a PRIMEd individual.

> "… If we wait for the moment when everything, absolutely everything is ready, we shall never begin."
> *Millan*

You should never put so many conditions on yourself to achieve a goal that you talk yourself out of even beginning the process. A good example is when married couples are trying to decide when to start a family. It's pretty rare for anyone to be ready for what parenthood brings to their lives. So many things should be accomplished beforehand that it's easy to put it off indefinitely because the stars and planets are never aligned perfectly. Some want a house, a decent savings account, careers to be solid, to be a certain age, to have traveled together as a couple, to move to a more desirable location, etc., You must decide which things are major and minor goals and then some minor ones may have to be completed during pregnancy in order to complete them before the baby is born. Some may have to wait until after you become a parent, but you must seize those larger goals when they present themselves and adjust accordingly. Whatever works! Remember, this is a goal that is dependent on someone else – your spouse. If either of your careers requires travel then your time to work on "the business" of starting your family is even more challenging to begin with. Add that one to your list of obstacles to overcome.

Take chances but be smart about it. Make sure you have a plan for everything you do so you are making progress towards your goal. Taking chances is sometimes a good thing to do; on the other hand failure is unacceptable. Remember, if you take something on make sure its part of your PRIME and you will be succeed in the end.

> "Let the refining and improving of your own life
> keep you so busy that you have little time to
> criticize others."
> H. Jackson Brown

Dignity

For the life of us we cannot understand how people can suck up to executive management so blatantly. How can they face themselves in the mirror each day? Please don't go there. Spend the time doing quality work and communicate your efforts in the politically correct manner. Discipline will give you the strength to avoid brown-nosing. Because you now have values that you adhere to, they will keep you a safe distance away from this type of behavior. You'll feel better about yourself in the long run.

Everyone knows if you possess dignity or not. It's worth having if you value your reputation. Those undermining jerks that waste precious time badmouthing others are doing more damage to their own reputation. It shows a genuine lack of character and self-esteem on their part. Actions always speak louder than words. This is the quickest route to being labeled as a backstabber and someone who is not trustworthy. This stuff spreads like wildfire, don't kid yourself into thinking no one notices. When or we should say – if you progress in your career using this method you will be very lonely at the top and you'll always wonder why. If you had spent more of your time improving yourself instead of putting others down then you'd have a stellar reputation, be admired by everyone you met along the way and be welcomed with open arms and applauded by your peers when you reach the top. If you live a decent, happy life and work to make things better everyday you'll be admired. If you are constantly complaining about everything to everyone who will listen then you are a whiner. Trust us on this one. No one likes a whiner.

Harris writes: When I was in my mid to late twenties I was a young executive climbing the corporate ladder. One of the most common challenges I encountered was how to deal with and manage executive management. I did it on good work ethics and quality work. Many of my peers went the route of sucking up. Unfortunately they got further ahead than me but as I look back today I am a much happier person for sticking with my principles. I can look myself in the mirror everyday and know that I achieved my status using my mind and body connection (discipline) as opposed to relying on my social connections.

The BUF Factor

If we were to pick just three attributes for acquiring discipline that you absolutely had to have they would be: maintaining a sense of <u>Balance</u>, <u>Urgency</u>, and <u>Focus</u>. It may be acceptable though not optimal to have only urgency and focus. These two factors define the qualities of discipline. To succeed you need to have a sense of urgency 24 hours a day and never lose sight of your goals and priorities. Balance is difficult, but it will come in time.

Balance

"Remember to live"
Goethe

Do you think this doesn't seem like a balanced life? It may appear that way but in reality it's what you make of it. It's how you set your priorities. Whatever that balance is for you, i.e., family, exercise or fun, so be it. For others it may be career, golf, and football. Everyone is different and everyone has different priorities. But the bottom line is as long as you set your own priorities that work best for you, a balanced life will take shape.

Harris writes: My way of life is exciting and challenging for me. For me it's little sleep, little relaxation, exercise, travel, and many accomplishments. For some of you it could be two long vacations a year and a few accomplishments, for others it could be family time, career, partying, etc.

My life is balanced – just the way I want it. Based on your goals and priorities you can have that balanced life as well. But to have a balanced life you <u>must</u> be disciplined. Now remember if you want it all (i.e. 5 or 6 different priorities) – forget it, none of us can have it all and if you try you will be stuck in mediocre bliss. It's a much better balance if you focus on fewer things and do them very well than to stretch yourself thin and not do any of them well.

Now that I've accomplished so much do I want to take it easy a bit? Do I want to relax and take more vacations? Not really, to me it's a waste of time. To me one vacation a year is sufficient. Too much time off doesn't do anything for me I'd rather be working on a new project. You might ask what about quality time with your family? That's built into my priorities but when we go on vacation – after everyone's asleep – I'll be busy working on my laptop computer. Accomplishments are fulfilling for me. I view relaxation as just a temporary feeling. I make time for relaxation, but in very small increments because that's how I benefit the most from it.

Sense of Urgency

"Even if you are on the right track, you'll get run over if you just sit there"
Will Rogers

Time doesn't slow down or stop and wait for you to get your act together. Time is running out so you need to start making something happen with your life. There should be a sense of urgency with every day of the year (see Chapter 6: Most Frequently Used Excuses; Complacency).

How do you view the following quote? "Tomorrow is another day". If you've had one of those "Groundhog Days" when absolutely everything is going wrong and bad news abounds then it gives you hope that tomorrow will be better. This is how it's meant to be taken. Unfortunately, everyone looks at things differently so some view it as an excuse to be lazy and this becomes their mantra. It's the opposite of saying, "Why put off until tomorrow what I can do today?" Why waste the most precious resource you have - time? It will never come back and if you keep procrastinating you will never succeed in completing your goals on schedule.

Those of us who apply the BUF factor to our lives are the ones who are always on the move. We have a tendency to walk and talk fast. We can't help it, that's our urgency in action. Karen writes: I will never forget an observation made by an Icelandic friend of mine, Hafstein Hafsteinsson, who I worked with at the Naval Air Station Safety Office in Keflavik, Iceland. He asked, "Do you realize that you are always leaning forward when you walk?" I joked that it was probably the result of walking in hurricane force winds on a regular basis compliments of their unforgiving weather. I thanked him for pointing that out to me because I don't make a habit of watching myself walk. We both were always rushing around the office and elsewhere because we had that sense of urgency in common. This accelerated walking was never more appreciated than when I made impromptu Klondike Bar runs for the office.

Focus

> "The ability to concentrate and to use your time well is everything."
> *Lee Iacocca*

We think this is the most difficult attribute of the three required to be "in the BUF." No matter how you choose to look at it, it's a great place to be. This is why those home projects never get completed and why there is never enough time in a day. Instead of focusing on goals, those other little things "that only take a minute" keep compounding until nothing ever gets finished.

Karen writes: This is the reason why I have always been much happier being on my own doing just about anything, as opposed to joining a group. I've watched and learned that the larger the group, the greater the potential for losing focus of what the group is getting together for in the first place. No one has a problem changing plans on a whim and everyone else will follow like sheep so as not to disrupt the flock. Before you know it the entire flock is at odds with each other and their time is being spent working out their differences instead of focusing on much more important issues in their lives that warrant their attention. They waste time worrying about what the other sheep think of them so they dare not leave the flock now! So the entire group continues this vicious cycle of disturbing behavior as scheduled.

If you enjoy groups and they enhance your life then go for it. If you waste countless hours complaining about it, then get out or change groups. Focus on what you are really looking for. Another example is the one we've all heard a gazillion times. If you're a looking for a spouse then do what you love and you will find someone who shares your passion. If you frequent the bar scene then you're probably more into dating than marriage. Focus on what is really important to you, not what's important to everyone else.

Don't be like everyone else. Don't worry about what everyone else is doing. To get nowhere, follow the crowd.

> "Often we allow ourselves to be upset by small things we should despise and forget. We lose many irreplaceable hours brooding over grievances that, in a year's time, will be forgotten by us and by everybody. No, let us devote our life to worthwhile actions and feelings, to great thoughts, real affections and enduring undertakings."
> *Andre Maurois*

Don't be upset with minor grievances and disputes. It will be a fulltime job just staying on top of your goals. You have your PRIME, now focus and concentrate on execution. You have to decide if it's worth your time. In most cases you'll find that its not. Don't waste your time rehashing incidents that you can't control. You can't change someone else's behavior, so move on. On the other hand, if something is really bothering most of us we feel better if we discuss it so we can then move on with a clear conscious. It's never a good idea to make assumptions or let things fester because sooner or later you're going to explode. For you Seinfeld fans, "Serenity Now!" doesn't work. The clean-up time required after that explosion is significantly longer than time spent averting such a mess. Don't look back. You're a one-person act.

Keeping Your Cool

"Nothing gives one person so much advantage over another as to remain always cool and unruffled under all circumstances."
Thomas Jefferson

One of the biggest obstacles you'll face as you're attempting to acquire discipline is keeping your cool. We've all been in those situations when someone ruffles your feathers for one reason or another.

Don't waste precious time on these types of individuals. Be creative and find ways to bypass the problem. You will be so focused on your goals and priorities that there will be very little time for anger or hatred towards something or someone. Not only is this a waste of precious time, but it's detrimental to your health and well-being. Avoid it at all costs. You have much better things to do with your life.

"Speak when you're angry, and you'll make the best speech you'll ever regret."
Lawrence J. Peter

Hope

It's great to be hopeful about things in life. It's definitely better than feeling hopeless, no doubt. There are times when hope is all you have to hold onto when circumstances are totally out of your hands. After you've exhausted every option and done everything you could possibly do, then there's always hope as a last resort. When you're dealing with serious medical conditions in your family, sending your child off to college or hearing from a friend who was just diagnosed with a disease you always hope and pray for the best.

For some people it's not about those situations that are out of their control. They are always hoping things will happen instead of making them happen. They are spending too much time hoping and not enough time doing things to reach their desired outcome. Hope can't help you accomplish things and become successful. People waste too much time and energy hoping for things to change or happen for them. You can't change the weather, but you can prepare for it and make alternate plans if you're planning an outdoor event.

Karen says, "My Mom has been reciting the Serenity Prayer ever since I can remember. It goes like this; God grant me the serenity to accept the things I cannot change, the courage to change the things I can and the wisdom to know the difference. Those are words to live by."

Don't hope for things that are obviously in your control. Make things happen, don't sit around and hope they will. You need to create and control your own destiny using your PRIME. It's all about gaining control. Once you've done that, then feeling hopeless or being hopeful about accomplishments will be behaviors of the past. You will know things will happen without a shadow of a doubt and that is extremely invigorating.

The Negative Side Affect

There are two distinct things that will take place when you're disciplined. We've already mentioned being restless and not wanting to sit around doing anything that you would consider a waste of your time. Work on your PRIME until you are scheduling that time to enjoy. If you begin to replace your relaxing time with other things you will regret it. You must live each and every moment so you are truly living in that moment and enjoying it – not thinking about other things you need to do. This is what PRIME does for you. It's focusing with all you've got on the goal ahead of you. This is especially important when you're spending time with your kids. They know if you're there mentally, physically or both so don't shortchange them because you've failed to "fit them into your schedule." Give each one of your tasks your full and undivided attention.

This other side affect is totally out of your control, but we guarantee you that it will happen repeatedly. Beware the green-eyed monster. Karen writes: For me that monster first reared its ugly head when I was 6 and has continued to appear in various forms to this day. A neighbor girl in my class was telling everyone not to like me, telling lies, etc. I still remember approaching her on the playground and asking her why she was doing that. She said, "You have pretty hair and everyone likes you!" I felt sorry for her and thought maybe she just needed a friend so I did my best to be one. But I kept my distance and never trusted her and so goes the politics of first grade and life. Later in life I realized that it was much more about having discipline than nice hair, but having both can be very threatening to a lot of people. Most especially to people who don't have either of those things!

People are very competitive. Your true friends will be happy for you when you achieve milestones in life. But if you're the type who has the discipline to continue this pace throughout life you will lose favor with many of those who don't have those attributes. We think it also reinforces how important positive vs. negative thinking is. Are you genuinely happy when a friend is doing well, or are you so insecure that you react negatively to the news?

It will suck at times; we're not going to lie to you. You have to realize that the reason these undisciplined people are envious is because their life sucks, not yours. But are you going to stay at their level or rise above it to become the best person you can be? Whose happiness is at stake here? They are jealous, they usually don't understand why, but we'll be the first to admit that we love getting "I wish I could do that" looks from people. It reminds us that we are doing something that is very uncommon (unfortunately) and envied. Those jealous ones are showing their negative attitude and you know how we feel about that. We always gravitate towards positive people because we can't tolerate people who are endlessly focusing on the negative aspects of their life. Its a waste of their time and we will not allow them to waste our time unless we see a serious effort on their part to create change for themselves.

I have been making this point for years and feel very strongly about it. Jealousy is the root of evil. My opinion was recently solidified in a Parade Magazine commentary in the Ask Marilyn column. Marilyn Vos Savant is in the Hall of Fame for "Highest IQ" so I'm in good company on this one. A reader asked, "What do you think is the source of evil?" Here's part of Marilyn's response; Reprinted with permission from PARADE, copyright © 2002. "In my opinion, evil often begins with jealousy. An edifice is then built to house that jealousy, an unconscious effort to deny this humiliating emotion: The individual finds a section of writing or constructs a forum, hoping to win converts. As the group grows, obsession may result. If it does, and the object of jealousy remains unfazed, hatred may take root."

I am no Marilyn, but I am motivated by my passion and fueled by my common sense and positive attitude. As for Marilyn, I'm sure she has had her fair share of dealings with the monster too because, you know, she's got such great hair.

4. TIME

"Time is the scarcest resource and unless it is managed nothing else can be managed."
Peter F. Drucker

Peter Drucker hit the nail right on the head. How many people do you know of that manage their life down to the minute? We bet none. Did you ever stop to think why people always run out of time at the end of the day? Rarely do they get everything done for any given day. These day's time <u>must</u> be managed to get as many things done as possible in a 24-hour period.

Equate Time To Money

"Don't say you don't have enough time. You have exactly the same number of hours per day that were given to Helen Keller, Pasteur, Michaelangelo, Mother Teresa, Leonardo da Vinci, Thomas Jefferson, and Albert Einstein."
H. Jackson Brown

Why in the world would anyone equate time to money? A very simple answer, one third of your lifetime is spent working. Your employer pays you a salary based on your skills, experience, hard work, and dedication. One third for most of you is spent sleeping. The other third is what you make of it. It's your time but unfortunately time is limited and sooner or later you will die - that's a guarantee.

"Lost wealth may be replaced by industry, lost knowledge by study, lost health by temperature or medicine, but lost time is gone forever."
Samuel Smiles

Life is too short and while you're on this planet why not get the most out of it? We equate time to money because time is precious and scarce. Most people don't like to throw money away because it takes too much time and effort to earn it. In our society you won't get very far without money. So if our time is scarce and precious the only logical thing to do is equate every minute with some monetary value. Every minute should have a price tag associated with it. Not every hour, but **every** minute. This analogy forces us to realize how valuable time is and to stop wasting this priceless resource as of right now. We promise you that your time could not be better spent than reading what follows.

By far the number one excuse people share with us is that they don't have enough time on any given day. We beg to differ because Tables 2.3 – 2.9 paint a totally different picture. It highlights how much time people waste on any given day. If you take a hard look and write down your daily schedule you'll see how much time in hours, not minutes, you actually waste each day (see Table 2.17). Associating a price for a day or a month won't cut it, but for every minute of your existence. How much time can you afford to throw away?

> "You may delay, but time will not."
> *Benjamin Franklin*

How much is a minute worth to you? Harris set his price tag at $10.00 a minute. Why $10.00? He wanted a hefty price tag associated with each day (A day equates to 1440 minutes). You only have so many days in a lifetime, can you really afford to waste those precious minutes? To get the most out of your life and accomplish more in a 24-hour period than you ever dreamt possible you <u>need</u> to associate a price tag to every minute of your life.

The following <u>is</u> reality:

Imagine. . . .

There is a bank that credits your account each morning with $86,400. It carries over no balance from day to day. Every evening deletes whatever part of the balance you failed to use during the day. What would you do? Draw out ALL OF IT, of course!

Each of us has such a bank. Its name is TIME. Every morning, it credits you with 86,400 seconds. Every night it writes off, as lost, whatever of this you have failed to invest to good purpose. It carries over no balance. It allows no overdraft.

Each day it opens a new account for you. Each night it burns the remains of the day. If you fail to use the day's deposits, the loss is yours.

There is no going back. There is no drawing against the "tomorrow." You must live in the present on today's deposits. Invest it so as to get from it the utmost in health, happiness, and success! The clock is running. Make the most of today.

To realize the value of ONE YEAR, ask a student who failed a grade.

To realize the value of ONE MONTH, ask a mother who gave birth to a premature baby.

To realize the value of ONE WEEK, ask the editor of a weekly newspaper.

To realize the value of ONE HOUR, ask the lovers who are waiting to meet.

To realize the value of ONE MINUTE, ask a person who missed the train.

To realize the value of ONE-SECOND, ask a person who just avoided an accident.

To realize the value of ONE MILLISECOND, ask the person who won a silver medal in the Olympics.

Treasure every moment that you have! And treasure it more because you shared it with someone special, special enough to spend your time.

And remember that time waits for no one. Yesterday is history. Tomorrow is a mystery. Today is a gift. That's why it's called the present!

> "You will never find the time for anything. If you want time you must make it."
> By: Charles Buxton

Don't Sit Around Wasting Time

> "The great French Marshall Lyautey once asked his gardener to plant a tree. The gardener objected that the tree was slow growing and would not reach maturity for 100 years. The Marshall replied, "In that case, there is no time to lose; plant it this afternoon!"
> *John F. Kennedy*

Every minute counts, especially when you're trying to get ahead of the game and accomplish so much in life. There are many instances where we can look back and see where we threw away valuable minutes which added up to hours, days or even months. That wasted time could have been used to turn some of your dreams into reality. Twenty or thirty years ago there wasn't as much pressure to do so much in such little time. We had the luxury of sitting around doing nothing whenever we had the opportunity. In most instances nothing was that urgent. Times have changed. Perhaps it's because of the incredible pace of technology, corporate competition, the economy, etc. The era of doing more with less is here to stay.

If we were sitting around in a doctor or dentist's office and waiting around for 20-30 minutes or even an hour for our appointment – who cared, we just picked up a magazine and started reading. Another example is when you go and get a haircut, although in most instances you probably have an appointment but on many occasions you would have to wait if your stylist was running a bit late. The same thing happens when you take your car into a mechanic, you could sit there for half a day. But in the twentieth century it wasn't as big a deal as it is now. On more occasions you had the luxury of sitting around and doing nothing.

Can you really afford to sit around and do nothing in this era? We don't think so. Always be prepared. Bring along some of your work – whatever that may be. We bring our laptop computers whenever we go to appointments. If there is no wait – so be it, then we haven't wasted our time. But at least we're prepared if they're behind schedule. Even if you don't own a laptop, bring along a book you've been wanting to read. You can even start writing a book, do your school work, or just bring along a pad of paper to take some notes of tasks you need get done or think of more creative ways to complete your goals ahead of schedule.

The sooner you can train the mind to equate every minute to money the sooner you start accomplishing more than you ever thought possible. Things you never had the time for. In any given year if you add all the time you were waiting around twiddling your thumbs waiting for appointments they would probably add up to several days. Table 4.1 below highlights some examples of where you currently sit around wasting precious minutes/hours and what our recommendations are:

> "What is a thousand years? Time is short for one who thinks, endless for one who yearns."
> *Alain*

Table 4.1: Time Wasters vs. Time Savers

Time Wasters	vs.	Time Savers
Government establishments (i.e., Department of Motor Vehicles, Court, Post Office, etc.,) – We all know that government offices are notorious for their bureaucratic and slow ways. Everything takes forever.		➤ Never go to one of these offices without bringing something along to read. Bring something to do, i.e., complete grocery lists, read books with your child, organize your schedule or balance your checkbook, etc.
On an airplane – 80% of the people are doing absolutely nothing for hours.		➤ Never leave without numerous options for keeping your kids and yourself busy. Everyone will benefit.
At an airport – especially after the 9/11 tragedy since you need to be at airports earlier – I travel every week and all I see is people sitting around staring at other people or walls.		➤ Always - yeah you guessed it, read, write, and work!
Auto mechanic – people sit around for hours.		➤ If you don't have things that are portable to do at the mechanics, then schedule your appointment & use their shuttle service so you can get on with your day.
Bus/Subway – traveling time		➤ Remember, half the luxury of traveling this way is having someone else drive, so make the best of it. Listen to music or books on tape while reading the newspaper or whatever you prefer.

Doctor's/Dentist's appointments	➢ Always be prepared. Bring along some reading material. You never know how long the wait will be or what emergency will walk into the office.

Treat All Days Equally

> "Being rich is having money; being wealthy is having time."
> *Margaret Bonnano*

Karen writes: Be mindful of the fact that a Monday or Friday is just as important as any other workday where discipline is concerned. Some use the days of the week as an excuse to be non-productive and this is a prime example of it. A lot of people are accustomed to running their minds on idle these days. Those who go the extra mile to complete projects on occasional weekends are getting 6 full days of productivity as opposed to the 3 days that the non-productive person gives. Promotions and opportunities will arrive twice as fast too and the others will be left scratching their heads and asking why they never progress.

The following is one of those funny office memos we all enjoy. We have found that some have used it more as a guide and we suspect that this is what they are doing with their Mondays and Fridays:

How to Kill 8 Hours a Day and Still Keep Your Job

It isn't that easy, but if you've got an average mind and a vague, ill-defined sense of resentment, you should be able to follow this easy guide to get away with it.

Minimum Daily Requirements
- A desk situated so you can escape scrutiny
- A window to stare out of
- A good acting ability

Things You Can Do Without Moving a Muscle

- Watch the clock
- Hum tunelessly
- Daydream
- Stare out into space
- Stew in your own juices
- Take a breather
- Sigh

It's Always Time For a Coffee Break!
- Check to see if there is any coffee brewing
- Return to desk to get cup
- Rinse out cup
- Pour coffee
- Blow on it
- Sip slowly

Coffee Break Projects
- Watch greasy film at surface of coffee swirl around
- Make weird patterns in Styrofoam cup with thumbnail
- Let it get too cold so you have a reason to walk to the microwave
- Strike up conversations with others on perpetual coffee breaks at microwave

Bored?
- Xerox your hand
- Think about old times
- Start vicious rumors about a co-worker

Make Your Own Office Toys
- With pushpins and a large eraser you can make a little pig
- A paperclip can become a modern mini sculpture
- Make and sail paper airplanes

Don't Forget to Doodle!
Have You Checked Out the Restroom Lately?
Never Just Wander Around. Have a Piece of Paper in Your Hand and Look Like You're Going Somewhere.
Look Annoyed So Everyone Thinks You're Stressed Out & Need a Break

Handy Hints! Easy & Fun!

- Clip fingernails
- Paint fingernails
- Bite fingernails
- Memorize calorie chart
- Unwrap and chew gum
- Swivel head on neck

For a Change of Pace, Organize Frequent Little Office Birthday Parties!!

Make sure everyone else is just as slow as you are. A consistent "we're all in this together" attitude can inspire you all to depths of sloth and inefficiency you never knew existed. It's easy!!

The funniest and saddest thing about the above memo is that we all have worked with people who actually do this stuff. If you are one of those people you better not be reading this at work!

I worked at a healthcare company that made the mistake of allowing only its home office employees the luxury of working half days on Fridays. Their mistake was not providing this incentive to all its offices. It caused resentment. It made the lazy employees lazier and the fast-movers slower on Fridays because they couldn't work with headquarters on those days. When they eventually did offer this option to everyone the result was typical. The sloths began their weekend attitude on Thursdays and the hard chargers worked as long as it took on Fridays because having a quiet workplace to yourself is very productive. It provided me with a wonderful incentive for my subordinates to finish their projects or forfeit their early Friday that week. We all won.

Weekends are meant to give us a break, but that doesn't mean you should turn into a couch spud. Have planned activities and things to accomplish around the house when you're not relaxing. Would your time be better spent getting ahead on a project or watching a TV program that interests your spouse while simultaneously putting you to sleep? Your time is equally important every single day of the week. How you spend your weekends says a lot about you and what you value in your life. If they are reflecting the opposite of what you say is important, then its time to put your money where your mouth is.

"Do what you can with what you have where you are."
Theodore Roosevelt

With every new location we settle in comes the inevitable observations from locals. Our time is limited until a new assignment requires us to move again. Since we never know exactly how much time we will be in each city we make the best of it by being avid local tourists. People who have lived there all their lives take it for granted and often choose not to rediscover their surroundings. All it takes is some planning and driving, but they are simply amazed at how much we accomplish on our weekends. They always ask, because they know we're always going somewhere and doing something fun. They just don't make it happen nearly as often. After all, reading up on local events and planning takes time. Most are content to take our advice and go the very same places after hearing of our adventures. Imitation is the sincerest form of flattery, but there is something very valuable to be learned here.

> **"Bloom where you are planted."**
> **Nancy Reader Campion's Aunt Grace**

If we did not have the roving lifestyle we do we may not be motivated to explore our surroundings as vigorously either. Knowing that our time is always finite keeps us moving to do as much as possible because we will never have a chance to be local and have that luxury again. This is how our mini vacation weekends came to be. Having to move often is not fun or easy, but you better believe that we always take full advantage of our time between those dreaded moves. We don't care what day of the week it is!

Standing in Line

Karen writes: This one never ceases to amaze me. Consider for a minute how many times we do this. Now, think about ways that we could've avoided it. When it can't be avoided, how can you benefit from this gridlock to accomplish things? It's as simple as calling ahead or using the Internet to purchase tickets for events or even movies. Don't be a line dog.

I love a killer sale as much as anyone but I refuse to stand in a line when I don't have to. My time is usually more valuable than the savings I reap. Those times when everyone is flocking to the stores is not the best use of your time unless you are creative about getting out of there quickly. Why do women waste their time doing this? I will go to the nearest register that has no line and trust me, there are usually plenty. It won't be anywhere close to where the women are but I'll hotfoot it downstairs. Why? Men don't flock to the stores for sales. They don't even spend their time shopping at all if it can be avoided. Men's stuff is usually downstairs and you'll find it quite peaceful, the cashiers are generally bored and thrilled to have something to do. Being able to save your family money and yourself time is what you should always try to do. That whole money/time combo is very sweet!

If All Else Fails, Work That Line!

Karen writes: If you're in a store and you know you're going to get a lot of things then get a cart or basket. This will keep your hands free so you can do something else. I don't care if its organizing your purse, calling someone on your cell phone or updating your electronic planner, you can't do much if your hands are full in a long line.

I shop in military commissaries that are busy just about anytime. All grocery stores are hectic, but you don't have to be there at the busiest times. We know never to go on or near a payday when it's a madhouse, so I plan accordingly. Go early or late when it's generally quiet to save time. There are still always lines, especially when it's a large base with a large retirement population. It can get very ugly. At some bases its not uncommon to stand in line for 30 minutes no matter when you go so its a variable that is worth some planning if this is the case for you.

Given all the above information, there are some things you can do. If you use coupons, verify them in line so you're not holding up the line with questions from the checker. The same goes for check writers; fill out everything you can prior to save time. When next in line offer to help the person in front of you by putting their groceries on the conveyor belt with them. When I am just standing there I prefer to help them than to watch them struggling to keep up with the cashier. It saves time for them, myself and everyone else. It's always a good feeling to help others and my daughter gets to see the benefits of doing that as a bonus.

When I'm up I place any coupons on the counter, tell the baggers beforehand what kind of bags I want and place everything so the barcodes are easily seen for scanning. It's ridiculous that they have to ask every customer the same question that we all know is coming. My daughter is 5 and she hands me things until the cart is empty enough for her to stand in it. Then she stands in the cart and can get her little hands on everything easier to hand to me. We've been doing this since she was 3. Not only do we both enjoy our grocery shopping together, but we also get a kick out of beating our time! I have my favorite speedy cashiers that we race with. David is the one who challenges us the most. He enlists the fastest baggers to gain every advantage in an attempt to swipe everything through quicker than we can keep up. One of them will set their watch timer to time us strictly for entertainment value. David only has one arm but he doesn't let that slow him down or stop him from having fun at his job. He's by far our favorite cashier.

There is no whining for the candy that is strategically placed at kids eye-level at the checkout. There is no time for that. Our goal is to get out of there quickly as possible so we can reward ourselves later with a trip to the park.

The World On Time

Karen writes: This is the FedEx slogan, but it's something we wish more people thought about too. If this was a reality, we'd all be generally happier in our existence. It's never just about our time, but you should also value the time of others. Who likes it when someone shows up late for a meeting, appointment or scheduled event? It shows total disrespect for that person's time. If time is as valuable as money, then do you really think that bodes well for your reputation? Don't waste other people's time. We don't care who you are; their time is as valuable as yours.

If people were all working in PRIME time, then the consensus would be that being late is unacceptable. Think about all the traffic fatalities that could be avoided because people weren't always late for something or other. We'd prefer policemen were spending less time writing speeding tickets to people who fail to schedule their time and more time catching criminals. Seems the world would be a better place for all of us if that were the case.

Any profession that relies on people to show up on time is nerve wracking! I worked in a hospital in various clinics for three years and people don't seem to value their health because showing up is somehow optional for them. Some believe that rules are made for everyone else. A lot of people took time to book the appointment, pull records, schedule and inform doctors, etc., all for nothing. That affects the entire schedule for the patients who follow that day, not to mention the office staff and the doctors themselves. Its sad how blatantly selfish people can be about other people's time. You can spend your time as you like, but other people's time is not for you to squander.

If you are a no-show for an appointment at an Air Force base this is handled in various ways, all which are dependent on your Command at the time. It is documented and will make its way to your Commander. You may receive verbal, written and administrative reprimands depending on the number of no-shows on your record. It's not a good thing in any case. Some Navy bases ask you to show up 15 minutes early when you are booking your appointment. If you don't make it by your appointment time, then you are out of luck and you will have to reschedule. It's too bad these rules have to be in place at all. They exist because a good portion of the population make a habit out of breaking commitments and their word to be there seems suggestive at best.

5.   <u>SLEEP</u>

> "Lost, yesterday, somewhere between sunrise and sunset, two golden hours, each set with sixty diamond minutes. No reward is offered for they are gone forever."
> *Horace Mann*

At first glance this doesn't appear to be something that would be considered a major timesaver. The truth is, this is so huge that it rated its own chapter. It is probably the most creative of them all. Being creative means going where no one else would go. We all steal hours away from our sleep schedules on occasion and that's pretty common. What we're suggesting is very uncommon, but we guarantee that it will spark an "Aha!" moment for the open-minded. Some may not be willing to be this creative, but then again, you probably just haven't given it much thought to begin with.

Minimizing Sleep

Harris writes: "I'm not very productive today, I didn't get my 8 hours of sleep last night". I've heard this one countless times. Who says you need 8 hours of sleep a night? Some doctors who write medical journals? How frequently do you see medical professionals in top-notch condition? Have they ever tried sleeping less than 6 hours a night for a long period of time? I don't think so. From the time I was a youngster it was continuously pontificated upon me that if I didn't get at least 8 hours of sleep I would get rundown and eventually get sick.

Techniques

If you eat properly and exercise consistently you will find out exactly how much sleep you really need for yourself. I cut my sleep down to 4 hours a night. We don't recommend this to anyone else. In order to cut back on your sleep you must eat right and exercise regularly. We can't stress this point enough! Not many people can honestly say they fit into this category. There is no reason why you can't experiment to find your minimum.

Figure out how much sleep your body needs to function at its optimum level. Average it out over a 4-6 week period and stick to it until it becomes habit. Tiredness in itself is a habit that can be broken. If you've been waking up early since childhood you're probably still doing that through force of habit. You've trained your mind and your internal clock is set based on repetition. Change your mind and your internal clock will automatically change with it.

If you want to cutback on your sleep you must take it gradually. You'll need to train your mind and body in the same way you would build endurance in the gym. Just think if you had an extra hour each day to do what you want. That extra hour will allow you to accomplish so much more than you ever thought possible. The fact that you gave up your sleep for it makes it that much more sacred. We guarantee you'll make the best of that additional time. When people ask me "Wouldn't you like to sleep a few extra hours?" My response is always the same. <u>I will sleep plenty when I die</u>. Hey, I'm human. There are days when I push myself so hard it warrants a 10--20 minute power nap if my schedule permits, of course.

Just get tough! Set the alarm earlier and get your lazy butt out of your bed. There's nothing else to it. If you do it everyday and don't hit the snooze button you'll get used to it. It might be difficult for the first few weeks. Just remind yourself of the things you could accomplish in that time. More importantly, start doing those things to fill that time as you are experimenting. Then you will immediately anticipate using that time to accomplish those goals.

Excessive Sleep

Why do some people sleep more than 8 hours? Everyone is different, but we're not talking about small amounts of time here. Some people get 6 hours and some always get 10. We think boredom is the culprit. If life isn't exciting or fulfilling then we get bored. We can't defend what we're saying rationally, but we believe it. If you're passionate about your purpose in life, then sleep is looked upon as something you must do for your physical and emotional health. In the morning you jump out of bed and can't wait to experience another day to it's fullest.

One of the signs of depression is excessive sleep. It's not that extra sleep is necessary, its more likely that sleeping through a difficult time is easier than facing reality. It provides an escape from life.

When We Can't Sleep

Karen writes: Why do we have trouble sleeping the night before that first day of school or when starting a new job? It's the excitement and anticipation of the next day. Sometimes your mind is so full of thoughts that it simply keeps on going, totally screwing any plans of sleeping you may have had. We've all been there, watching the clock wide-eyed until about 2 hours before you have to go to work. I quit fighting it years ago and just get out of bed and get busy doing something instead of wasting those hours tossing and turning in bed. Once your mind gets focused on something else, then you'll be able to get back to sleep sooner. The quality of your sleep will be better as a result. If you're unlucky like me, you spend the better part of those 2 hours dreaming about whatever you were thinking about, which seems more brutal than not having slept at all.

Killer Sleep Study

The University of California at San Diego (UCSD) released a sleep study in February 2002 that suggests that there is an increased death rate associated with sleeping 8 hours or more. Daniel Kripke is a UCSD professor of psychiatry and nationally known sleep researcher. He challenges recommendations from many health organizations including the National Sleep Foundation. The amount of sleep required to maintain good health is less than 8 hours.

Although it's a common belief that 8 hours of sleep is required for optimal health, a six-year study of more than one million adults ages 30 to 102 has shown that people who get only 6 to 7 hours a night have a lower death rate. Individuals who sleep 8 hours or more, or less than 4 hours a night, were shown to have a significantly increased death rate compared to those who averaged 6 to 7 hours.

According to his study published in the February issue of the Archives of General Psychiatry titled, "Sleep less, live longer?" findings showed that those who slept 8 hours were 12 percent more likely to die within the six-year period of the study than those sleeping 7 hours. The 8-hour sleepers were 4 to 5 percent more likely to die than those sleeping six hours. Even those with as little as five hours sleep lived longer than participants getting eight hours or more per night. The best survival rates were found among those who slept 6.5 to 7 hours per night.

Kripke stated, "Our data show that people need sleep only the amount they need to feel well-rested, at least down to about 4 hours a night. We don't know if long sleep periods lead to death." In a KUSI TV interview Kripke said, "This does not mean that you should set your clocks earlier. It does mean that if you feel rested with 6.5 hours, you do not need 8 hours to be healthy."

Although the study was conducted from 1982-88, the sleep results have not been available until recently due to the length of time required to input and analyze the vast amount and variety of data from the 1.1 million participants. The variables that were taken into consideration were age, diet, exercise, smoking and previous health problems that influenced mortality statistics.

Make It A Goal

Harris writes: I treat sleep as a goal, as opposed to a physical necessity just because people say you need a certain number of hours of sleep a night. When I was in my early twenties I slept 8 hours a night on weekdays and 10 hours a night on weekends. I was no different than any other teenager. As I was acquiring discipline my confidence was growing along with my list of goals. I decided that sleep was a waste of time because I had too many things I wanted to accomplish.

I established a goal to cut my sleep down gradually (an hour at a time) until I was able to get my sleep down to 4 hours every night. It was a very aggressive goal and I didn't know how my body would react so I went slowly. Every time I cut back on my sleep for an hour I would give my body 3-4 weeks to adjust before taking on anymore. Why 4 hours? I really don't know, but it's worked for over 20 years now.

Sleep is a necessity and requirement but the amount of sleep is something you can play with. Tell your mind it's just a number and nothing more and that too much sleep is a waste of time. Repetition is important again here.

For myself and I think for many people out there it's fun to challenge yourself with numbers:

> ➢ *With your salary at work – how high can I go?*
> ➢ *With weightlifting - how much weight can I lift?*
> ➢ *With field and track events – how many seconds can I shave off my time – how low can I go?*

Playing with numbers is fun. So why can't we play with the number of hours we sleep? You can and that's exactly what I've been doing for the past 3 decades. Train that mind to drive those numbers down to your bare minimum! If you feel rested and you're productive during the day, then you know you've got it right."

We're Not Alone

Anyone who has been through military basic training can confirm the effectiveness of minimum sleep coupled with physical conditioning. Sometimes its 2-3 hours a night for up to 6 weeks. Not only do recruits survive the experience, they are forced to realize what they are capable of accomplishing. It's only temporary for them, but it's a full-time job for their drill instructors. Have you ever seen a Marine Drill Instructor (DI)? They all look like any Marine ad or poster you've ever seen. The DI's and their recruits running cadence behind them are alert and in the best shape of their life. Being kept on a strict regimen of minimum sleep has enhanced their lives - forever.

Statistics show that about 20 percent of Americans are employed in some kind of shift work. Too many to list here, but some that come to mind are the transportation industry, food industry and the military. Some do work that requires an extremely high degree of concentration. Submariners and air traffic controllers are a couple of them.

The Naval Submarine Medical Research Laboratory performs watch-standing studies. They have experimented with all kinds of alternative watch and sleep schedules to increase operational performance as well as better the quality of life for submariners. They have examined what is best to suit their function. Everyone should toy with this concept to streamline sleep schedules for themselves. Whether you're a genuine Navy submariner or an avid submarine sandwich eater you can do this.

Extensive research has also been done on air traffic controllers. Research on 37 air traffic controllers in Jacksonville found that those whose frequent shift changes included the after-midnight graveyard shift were better able to focus on the tasks at hand during the day, said Raymon McAdaragh, who did the study for his doctorate at The University of Florida at Jacksonville in instruction and curriculum. "What I learned is the opposite of what you would expect. People on rapidly rotating schedules that include graveyard shift have better attention allocation, quicker reaction times and are better able to learn cognitive tasks during the day shift."

The point is, there are variables that are not being utilized because no one bothered to do the research. We can learn from others who already realize that sleep is an adjustable option that is well worth further exploration.

> "Time is the most valuable thing a man can spend."
> *Diogenes Laetius*

6.   TRAINING THE MIND

> "Man's mind stretched to a new idea never goes
> back to its original dimensions."
> *Oliver Wendell Holmse*

You have a plan (PRIME), now go make it happen! If it were that easy we wouldn't be writing this book. The most difficult part throughout this entire process is to push and motivate yourself <u>everyday</u> of the year. The only way to drive yourself consistently is to train the mind to push your body for you. Once you train the mind to be that guiding force behind all your actions then and <u>only</u> then will you become successful. It will constantly nudge you forward even when you're tired and feeling lazy. If you attempt to move forward and try to acquire discipline without properly training the mind then you will surely fail.

> "A closed mind is a dying mind."
> *Edna Ferber*

Train your mind by being repetitive. You now have an established set of priorities and a new daily routine. You need to eat, breathe, and live these priorities. Keep saying them over and over again in your mind. Repeat them at least a half dozen times each day. You cannot let one day go by without talking to yourself and addressing your priorities. As we were acquiring discipline in our teenage years there wasn't a day that went by that we didn't talk to ourselves about our priorities. Always complete your priorities first. <u>Never</u> procrastinate or deviate. You need to tell yourself that there is no tomorrow. Never push your priorities off until the next day regardless of the situation you may be in or the hardship it may cause. There may be obstacles or hurdles, but there can be no deviation from your plan.

Once your mind is trained the execution is automatic because the mind takes over and adheres to your priorities. The mind will be set to autopilot. If you try to disengage autopilot forget it – it won't let you. Your mind is now controlling your body as it does ours everyday.

> "One's mind has a way of making itself up in the
> background, and it suddenly becomes clear
> what one means to do."

A.C. Benson

In order to acquire discipline your mind has to be your guiding force. We'll probably say it a dozen times throughout this book because it bears repeating; your mind is the best tool and greatest asset you have to acquire discipline. Use it wisely and regularly to help you gain discipline, but more importantly to get ahead.

Your mind will rarely get tired or need a break, so take advantage of it. When acquiring discipline you need every tool you can get your hands on. The sooner you harness its strength to work in your favor the better. Then the sky is the limit.

Is it hard work? Without a doubt it's very hard work. Nothing this rewarding will be easy. Will it ever let you ease up? Sometimes but only after your priorities have been completed for that day. Don't think of this as a hobby or a side job. It's a full-time commitment. There are no breaks because you've trained your mind so well. It follows the business plan precisely and effectively.

Does your mind ever give up? No, because it knows the limitations you've laid out in your PRIME. Persistence is what it knows best. Nothing is as consistent as your mind. It will find innovative ways to accomplish goals. There is more than one way to complete a goal. It will find every avenue to assist you in accomplishing each and every goal. The answer to completing a goal is not always straightforward. It will always be thinking around the clock of different approaches to accomplishing your goals.

Playing Mind Games

Harris writes: I've been playing mind games to properly train my mind for over three decades. It has proven to be my greatest ally in becoming successful. Mind games are little things you say over and over again until these phrases become permanently entrenched in your mind and become part of your life. Silly as it may sound, they are the main ingredients to help you accomplish your goals. They may sound crazy and ridiculous, but it works! People often ask me what my secret formula is for acquiring discipline and accomplishing so much in life. I tell them that I talk to my mind and it talks to me all day long. Yes, its only one voice, and no I'm not schizophrenic!

It's so much more than training my mind to guide me when I need it the most. These little phrases are automatically and subconsciously played back in my mind at appropriate times repeatedly. The appropriate time is when you need that little extra push to help you accomplish the priorities for any given day. My mind doesn't speak to me in a soft gentle voice. It's more like a drill sergeant's voice never letting up and continuously bombarding me 24/7. The Sergeant is relentless – he never tires. My mind is no different. It never eases up or gives me a break. It's unyielding to guarantee my success. Maybe I trained it too well. As I previously mentioned I have been labeled a machine in my pursuit of accomplishments. But others also know without a doubt that I am a sensitive and caring individual as well. They know I am a man of my word and I will not waiver from accomplishing set goals. As I mentioned in my first book, with discipline comes values.

This sounds so farfetched, why should you believe me? I started with practically nothing. I barely passed high school, was pathetically skinny, and lived in a very poor neighborhood. Today I'm an author, publisher, executive, and family man with more accomplishments by the time I was 40 than most people would have in two lifetimes. I attribute it <u>all</u> to training the mind.

Yes, I still play mind games even at the age of 48 because it's the only way to effectively train the mind. The mind is your best tool to help you accomplish much more then you ever thought possible.

My greatest ally, companion, confidant, etc. is and always will be my mind. Please read the section titled: Most Frequently Used Excuses for a list of the most common reasons for not achieving discipline along with the mind games I played to overcome life's daily barriers.

Psyching Yourself Out is Child's Play

Karen writes: Since playing mind games is a habit around our house it's only natural that my 5 year old has become accustomed to doing it too. One of her friends told her that she was very sad because her Dad was going to be away for 2 weeks. My daughter replied, "Just tell yourself that it will be 3 weeks and before you know it he will be home!" She speaks from experience given my husband's job since we play that game a lot. We don't see this as silly at all.

It's just our way of putting a positive spin on a negative fact of our lives. We stay extremely busy, focus on the positive aspects of being able to hang out together and bond on our own terms. We do things that are special to both of us during those times so they become memorable experiences as opposed to sad ones.

Most Frequently Used Excuses

How many times a week do you use excuses as a reason for not completing a goal on schedule or not keeping a commitment? In this section we've documented some of the *most frequently used excuses* people use everyday. More importantly, we've documented the mind games Harris used to train his mind to combat these excuses. The solution isn't rocket science. It's really quite simple and may even seem corny, but there is a method to our madness, trust us! The solution is playing a mind game to train the mind to permanently erase excuses from your vocabulary.

Solutions For Those Excuses

1. I Have A Cold So I'll Take It Easy Today

We've all been there. When you're feeling ill and your energy level is running on empty, it's easy to keep telling yourself repeatedly that you should probably take it easy. Just about everyone else around you is telling you to take it easy too. After a while your mind starts coddling you and automatically tells your body to take it easy. You've trained your mind to react negatively by having it focus on your symptoms. This will rapidly accelerate your symptoms, so enjoy the ride because you're going down!

The average person gets two colds a year. As you know, a cold can last anywhere from a day to several weeks depending on the virus and severity. We've had our share of colds, especially being parents with young children. They just love bringing home the newest bug from school and sharing it equally among family members.

It's OK to take it easy when you're sick. As long as you don't have a fever, there is no reason to stay home from work or take a day off from exercise. You won't have as much energy as you normally would anyway. You're probably a bit uncomfortable with a few aches and pains, but so what? It won't harm you. It's important to apply some common sense and consider the health of your coworkers too. There's nothing worse than the person who comes to work when they are extremely ill. They are totally unproductive but manage to infect the entire office as well as their families.

Why sit around doing nothing, complaining, and feeling sorry for yourself? In the new millennium, no one has the luxury to sit around and do nothing. You're probably already doing the work of two people due to corporate layoffs, or because you have children and both parents are working. It's almost impossible to have extra hours for relaxation or personal downtime built into your busy schedule.

<u>Playing The Mind Game</u>

Get up and exercise a little, clean the house, or take a long walk. Just use some common sense and do things in moderation and don't over exert yourself. The point is to keep busy. Then cool down a bit and take a shower or a relaxing warm bath. You'll feel so much better both mentally and physically. Use your favorite remedies, i.e., chicken soup, hot tea, or cold medicine and get on with your day. Get up and stop wasting time hosting your own pity party. Make each minute of your life count.

When you catch a cold tell yourself that you're not sick repeatedly time and again. Reiterate in your mind that it's probably just a 24-hour bug. Regardless, the more you accomplish today the better off you'll be tomorrow. When tomorrow comes it's more of the same, except now it's a 48-hour bug. You get the idea. Think positively. Don't wimp out here! Tell yourself it's only temporary and you'll feel better tomorrow. Give your body what it needs to kick this cold's ass! Take care of it and it will take care of you. Those days when you're coughing, congested, and your throat is scratchy - push yourself that much harder to make things happen. Sure it may take more effort than usual but your body is busy fighting its own battle, so your mind must compensate. Don't just sit around doing nothing and become a couch potato.

Harris says, "When I have those same nagging symptoms people will ask me whether or not I am sick. My response has <u>always</u> been; 'Nope!' The point is not to let people feel sorry for you. If they start pampering you then you'll start babying yourself. Don't go there – stay mentally tough! Always challenge yourself to push that much harder when you're feeling down. You'll be rewarded by significantly reducing your 'down time' and feeling better sooner."

2. I Don't Feel Very Inspired Today - I'm Lazy. Maybe I'm Becoming Complacent In My Current Surroundings - Yes That's It, I Need A Change.

Rarely do physical surroundings negate you from achieving your goals. These feelings typically come from your mind and are inhibiting you from completing your goals on schedule. In most cases there are other issues you're going through (i.e., difficult times at work, or with your personal life, etc.) In that rare instance where your surroundings clearly do inhibit you from being productive then you must keep focusing on your goals and priorities. Eventually, after acquiring discipline you will have the ability and financial backing to do whatever you want, including relocation. Use the negative aspects of your situation as built-in motivators that push you on to achieving your goals.

Maybe you were up most of the night partying and you woke up very sluggish and had a headache. Everyone needs to live it up and have some fun - and occasionally indulge. We should also be able to sleep in a bit. Having some fun is not an excuse for telling yourself you're not inspired today. Sure you can relax a bit and be lazy for a few hours but that doesn't mean you need to take the entire day off and waste the day away. Save that luxury for a planned vacation so you can really enjoy yourself. Work hard and play hard.

<u>Playing The Mind Game</u>

Harris writes: Scare yourself into thinking that this year is your last year on earth. Do you want to sit around and vegetate or do you want to accomplish something? It sounds harsh and crazy, but it's very effective. I scared myself from my teens and well into my thirties that life would end for me at age 40. I kept training my mind day in and day out that I would never live past the age of 40. I even used to tell my friends the exact same thing. I started believing it myself and they did as well. When you think you only have so many years to live it's quite easy to feel inspired and to accomplish as much as possible. On the other hand, if you think you'll live until the age of 100 there's no sense of urgency or reason to feel inspired everyday.

It truly worked. All of my plans evolved around the age of 40. I had so much to accomplish and I had to do it by my 4th decade of existence. I took advantage of everyday I was alive. Now don't get me wrong, I wasn't trying to kill myself! I was just trying to train my mind that there was a sense of urgency, believing that everyday could be my last day and that I would be very lucky to hit the age of 40. It kept me focused and forced me to never take my life for granted. By the way, I accomplished all my goals by 40. I'm still alive, kicking, and accomplishing more goals at the age of 48.

Being inspired can be an everyday occurrence if your mind is properly trained. With PRIME and the efforts put forth in training your mind you'll have a reason to get out of bed each day of the year and to put that snooze button out of business once and for all. If you get up each day without a plan; then we don't blame you for not feeling inspired. You might as well stay in bed a few more hours hitting that "you snooze, you lose" button.

Do whatever works to inspire yourself <u>now</u>. It's very unfortunate that it takes a major life-changing event to shake most of us into inspiration. Creating your own inspiration is a significant life-changing event in itself.

3. I Am Overwhelmed And Feeling Stressed - I Can't Get My Work Done In 8 Hours - I Don't

Have The Time To Eat Healthy, Exercise, And To Spend Ample Time With My Family.

In 2002 feeling overwhelmed is a common occurrence. Your workload will continue to grow year after year. Balancing your life will be even more difficult. Everyone tries to do too much. But doing too much is normal these days. Work is a necessity as is family and friends and for some exercise and partying are more important. What is the right balance? Everyone is different and there isn't one right answer. Everyone wants to live their own life and get as much squeezed into a 24-hour period as possible. If you take on too much you'll be setting yourself up for a downfall. Once you've acquired discipline then it's OK to take on the world, but not in the early stages.

Harris writes: Develop your plan with the right combination of priorities. For me, it is family, career, health, and fun. The first three are a must on any given day. Everything else had to be put on the back burner. Fun was the bonus priority. If there was time, then so be it. Just in case you're wondering, there was time for fun, just not as frequent as some would like.

Once you have established your top 2-3 priorities then you must adhere to them at all times. In your mind you must eat, breathe, and live the rest of those priorities. Don't take on anymore and don't have more than 2-3 priorities total. There aren't enough hours in a day to take on everything. The more you try, the more you will fail and ultimately you will just get frustrated. It's important to get a taste of success early on in your endeavors. You NEVER want to fail, not even one time! I despise this quote; "it's OK to fail as long as you try". If you keep failing it becomes no big deal for you and it actually becomes routine. Don't <u>ever</u> go there. Yes, you should always try, but tell yourself instead that failure is not an option. This will make you work that much harder to do your very best to avoid it, instead of telling yourself that "failure is ok". Always be afraid of failure. Continuous failure breeds more failure causing a lack of confidence and self-esteem. On the other hand, meeting ongoing success builds upon these important traits with each success, which spurs you on to a life full of successful endeavors.

<u>Playing The Mind Game</u>

I spent every hour of everyday focusing on my goals. I kept telling myself over and over again that meeting my goal's scheduled completion date was a failure. It may seem silly and trivial, but I would go out of my way to complete a goal way ahead of my scheduled completion date. Never procrastinate. Always stay ahead of the game. You never know when an unplanned emergency will rear its ugly head. It's critical to build a buffer into your schedule especially for those unplanned emergencies.

I need to reiterate the importance of completing a goal ahead of schedule. Keep telling yourself repeatedly that meeting a goals completion date is not acceptable. I was training my mind to automatically push myself everyday to beat that deliverable. Call yourself every name in the book if that works for you (i.e., loser, failure, etc.). These were some of my favorites. If you're more motivated by humor then bonehead, dork and doofus come highly recommended. <u>Do whatever it takes</u> to beat that deliverable. You need to remember that <u>it's you against you</u>. Continuously challenge yourself and make it interesting so it's fun. It's like being in an arena and your enemies are your goals. <u>Beat them!</u>

4. I Can't Save Money And My Spending Habits Are Out Of Control.

You're not alone. Many people live their life from paycheck to paycheck. They struggle to keep up and never get ahead of the game. Their credit cards are usually maxed out and they pay only the minimum amount each month. They get so deep into debt that it's very difficult to get their heads above water. It's very important to work on and keep up with your fiscal fitness.

<u>Playing The Mind Game</u>

The answer is really quite simple. Saving money has to be a goal. It can't be an afterthought. Unfortunately millions of people consider saving money an afterthought. They wait until they're in their twenties, thirties, or even forties before they start thinking about saving money. This is a huge mistake that will be regretted for many years to come. They need to start learning about managing finances in their teens. A solid foundation on the value of money should be started as soon as kids can grasp the concept. What kids don't know about money can hurt them. The more they know, the more likely it is that they will become financially responsible adults. Who doesn't want a big savings account? Then all the more reason it needs to be a goal as early as possible. You must put future needs before present wants. Beginning is the hardest part. Once you begin, you'll never want to stop. Making your own security blanket goes a long way towards lowering stress that can be a deterrent to completing even the easiest goals.

If your goal is to save $100.00 every month, then why not make a check out to your savings account just as if you were making a check out to pay your monthly bills? If you pay 10 bills a month, what's one more? If $100.00 is too much, then be more conservative and go $50.00 or even $20.00 – whatever it takes and whatever is comfortable for you. It's important to make it a conservative amount or you will fail in your efforts to save money. If you're short on any given month, then you won't write this 11th check. In your mind you need to tell yourself that it's just like any other bill and you're paying it on the 1st of each month. Remember to always pay yourself first and saving money will never be a problem. It must be a priority, plain and simple.

The savings account has to be out of sight and out of mind just like a safety deposit box would be. Don't open up another checking account, as you'll have a tendency to go to it when things get a bit tight. It has to be a savings account. Harris says, "I had my regular checking account in one bank near my home and my savings in another several miles away. <u>Do not have easy access to your savings account!</u>"

The money in this savings account needs to be used to accomplish one of your goals whether it's a car, boat, home, or a vacation fund. Whatever you use it for, make sure it's for a significant goal and not for just a new watch, outfit or an impulse buy. Its best if it's for a goal that is something you need, but if it's for something that is just a want, be sure its something that is well worth your efforts. Case in point; if you're saving for a vacation make it to someplace that you've always dreamed about so it will be one that you'll never forget. Saving for a trip to Las Vegas and then gambling all your hard-earned money away is not a goal we'd recommend for someone who is struggling to save their money.

In several months you may want to increase the amount you save but you can never decrease it. That would mean your established goal would not be met. In other words, you've failed to acquire discipline! Once again it's important to stay very conservative in the beginning.

Harris says, "In 1967 I started with a minimum of $5.00 a week and gradually increased it on a consistent basis."

5. I Have A Hard Time Keeping My Commitments...

<u>If you can't keep them, don't make them.</u> Harris says, "I hate it when people make commitments on the spur of the moment. Commitments should be sacred and they need to be treated as such. It's easy to say 'yes' whenever convenient to appease someone. Your intentions are good because you have every intent in the world to help this person. The word intent means absolutely nothing to me. Any Tom, Dick, or Harry can have good intentions but what good is intent without action? You're doing harm to both parties by making commitments and never following through. If you know deep down that your odds of fulfilling your commitments are 50/50 at best – <u>please don't commit</u>."

Playing The Mind Game

The first step is to recognize the importance of keeping your word. Having discipline is so much more than just accomplishments or success, it's about values (see Chapter 7). Who doesn't want to be respected? Everyone wants to be respected. No one wants to be labeled a talker. If you keep on committing your time and not following through, we guarantee that you'll be labeled.

Harris says, "I've known so many people in my lifetime that I've negatively labeled. I could never respect or trust them. I used to ask myself, do I want to be labeled for the rest of my life? Once you're labeled it's difficult to remove it and chances are slim to none that you ever will. The game I played was to tell myself that I never wanted to be labeled a talker. All it takes is one time and watch how quickly you get labeled, regardless of the excuse."

Once you make a commitment for a friend then treat it as a goal, not just as a promise. If you're an individual that spends a lot of time helping your friends then you need to build this into your PRIME, where friends become one of your top priorities.

6. I Have Too Many Personal Problems To Worry About My Goals Right Now.

Harris writes: Personal problems (i.e., divorce, death in the family, etc.) are the most difficult to deal with. Nothing can slow you down more than these types of heartaches. I've been through a divorce. Nothing was more painful and devastating, especially when children are involved. Mentally it can destroy you for a very long time.

It becomes very difficult to motivate yourself when you're going through these major personal problems. You just feel like digging a hole and putting your head in it for a while.

Unfortunately emergencies can potentially knock you off your feet in more ways than one. Besides the mental anguish, there's the lack of motivation, emotional stress, goals become an afterthought and forget about work. Sometimes severe trauma can put someone out of commission for a very long time.

Playing The Mind Game

The simple mind game I play is telling myself everyday that there <u>will be</u> an emergency. Although I never want to have an emergency and in the 3+ decades I've been playing these mind games I've never had one - knock on wood – thank God! Unfortunately there's no other way but to be prepared mentally. No matter how much you prepare for it, the pain from a horrific emergency will still be there.

One of the comments I often hear is "So what if I can't accomplish my goals on schedule? I have an excuse, it's an emergency." Missing a goal's scheduled due date is not good practice. Once you do it, odds are you'll repeat it. On the same note, you can't ignore personal emergencies or pretend they'll never hit you or your family. It will undoubtedly paralyze you for quite sometime when it does unexpectedly occur.

When establishing your goals and priorities unplanned emergencies must be accounted for. Scare yourself - you need to be prepared. Training the mind to be prepared for an emergency will help you get over it that much quicker. Your mind will automatically remind you to focus on your priorities and goals ASAP. After a while you'll be prepared if, God forbid, something does happen. Your mind has been trained, which will expedite your recovery time. Your mind will not let you veer off course. It's the whole idea of focusing on the positive things in your life to help you deal with the negative ones. This is why keeping busy is even more important when disaster strikes so you don't allow your mind to become consumed with only the stress and/or sadness you are experiencing. Life goes on and dwelling on painful situations just prolongs the healing process. Time doesn't heal all wounds, but it certainly helps if you allow it to by making the very best use of it no matter what.

7. I'm Always Late For Appointments.

Harris says, "This has got to be one of the most common problems people have all over the world. Reasons are endless but the most common one is traffic. This is especially true if you live in a large metropolitan city. As I travel all over the world I see that traffic is definitely a problem, but being late for an appointment is no excuse."

Playing The Mind Game

Here's a very simple mind game we play: Tell yourself there will always be traffic or an accident and allocate your time accordingly. If you tell yourself to leave early then it won't be an issue. If the commute to your appointment without traffic is 30 minutes then leave one hour earlier. If you always double your commute time your odds of being late are slim to none. If you are chronically late and mind games don't work for you then it's time to take it up a notch. Set all your clocks and watches 10-15 minutes fast and never be late again.

Before you leave your house bring along reading material or your laptop computer just in case you do get there early. As we said earlier, time is money. There's no way you can sit there in the car 15-30 minutes early ahead of your scheduled appointment and do nothing.

8. I'm A Businessman And Travel 80% of The Time – I Don't Have The Time To Exercise And Eat Right Especially When I'm Traveling Overseas.

Harris says, "This excuse doesn't fly (pun intended) with me at all. I travel every week of the year. I'm always in an airport and on the go. It's astonishing to see how many young executives in their twenties, thirties, and forties that are so out of shape.

I hear the same old excuses:

> *I'm always tired when I arrive at my destination*
> *I get into my hotel at an unreasonable hour*
> *I'm too busy – need to get some work done on my computer when I get to the hotel room*
> *I'm too lazy right now – there's a three-hour time difference – it must be jet lag - I'll feel better tomorrow*

The list goes on and on.

What irks me is watching these out of shape excuse ridden executives walk through the airport with their luggage on wheels. Many of them even have their smaller briefcases on wheels. To make matters worse they take this luggage and stand on the automated walkways.

There are so many ways and opportunities to exercise before you even get on that plane. It would be wise to make it a goal since you know you're going to be sitting for several hours. And let's not forget about all that rich food you'll probably be eating.

Some of the biggest excuses I've ever heard were from these executives that complained how tired they were after traveling overseas. I'll have to admit it is an exhausting trip. So why not sleep a few hours on the plane?

I travel from Los Angeles to Singapore frequently. I would depart Los Angeles around noon on Saturday and arrive in Singapore around midnight on Sunday. I can understand being tired, but so what? I've never heard of someone dying from being tired. My mind would tell my body that I was tired just about every minute of the day if I allowed it to. My body does get tired and I need rest just like anyone else (just not as much). When you fly overseas it's almost impossible to sleep more than a few hours due to the time difference. Singapore is 16 hours ahead of Los Angeles. So why not get out of bed, turn the TV off and go to the hotel gym and exercise for 30 minutes? Most of the 4 and 5 star hotel gyms are open 24 hours a day. Once you complete your fitness routine you'll feel a hundred times better. What's 30 minutes? It's really not about being tired, it's just being lazy. Start walking through airports instead of using automated walkways. Forget the escalator; walk up the stairs to get your legs moving. Every little bit helps when you have a long flight to take. These little things add up. Stop being so lazy!

Playing The Mind Game

I kept telling myself that I was getting fatter and lazier each time I got on an airplane. Before you go on a long flight remind yourself that you are going to be sitting for hours stuffing your face with rich food and most likely having a few drinks. If you workout in preparation for travel you will feel better and be able to enjoy it knowing that you've taken care of your body. You deserve to relax, enjoy the flight and indulge in whatever the food cart brings your way. Since you already know traveling is tiresome in itself you must take advantage of every opportunity to stretch your legs, get your blood circulating and keep your mind busy according to your destination time if you can. Everyone knows how a heavy meal alone can induce instantaneous napping. It's asking for trouble to combine inactivity with rich food and then add a new timetable on top of it. Oh yeah, you're going to be feeling like crap for days. That's a shame since traveling can be much more rewarding if you are in good physical condition.

Another motivating factor for me is when people asked "How do you stay in such good shape when you travel so much?" You never tire of getting compliments about your health because you know how much discipline it requires to be in good shape. The fact that people notice and acknowledge the difficulty in spite of my hectic traveling schedule shows that not only do they admire my commitment, but they realize that it's not easy by any means. More importantly, it proves that it can be done if you play mind games to keep your health a constant priority even in the face of adversity.

9. I Can't Do It.

This has got to be the most exhausted excuse of them all. When things don't always go your way they're the easiest 4 words to use in the English language. It's easier to give up than to keep trying to overcome a particular barrier. Do you want accomplishments? Do you want to be successful? Do you <u>really</u> want some discipline in your life? Nothing worthwhile will come easy, whether it's that promotion or that special relationship you've always sought.

If you want it, <u>just do it</u>. But going after it without including it in your PRIME won't work. It has to be a goal, which fits into your priorities. Your priorities are fixed to help you accomplish all your goals. Don't just create new goals without putting the proper thought process behind them (i.e., looking at your current routine and priorities). Why do you think most New Years resolutions don't last past the first month? There's no substance behind the words. In most cases these resolutions were thought up on the spur of the moment. We like to use the phrase "Content Free Speech."

Harris says, "People who don't really know me will ask if I've made my New Years resolutions. Friends wouldn't dare ask because they know better. I tell the acquaintances who don't know me that there is no such thing as New Year's resolutions." If you make New Years resolutions the odds are pretty high that you will fail because it wasn't carefully thought out and there wasn't a formal plan supporting it.

Once you establish a goal then you know exactly what it takes to conquer that goal in your mind and you'll do <u>whatever it takes</u> to make that happen. If you rely on a certain event to attain a goal it's nothing more than a pipedream.

Playing The Mind Game

Tell yourself that failure is not an option. Remind yourself that if you fail even once you will always lack confidence to take on new challenges. Saying "I can't do it" is the equivalent of failure. Are you going to simply give up each time a new challenge comes along? Train your mind to be tough and to always persevere.

10. I'm Too Fat – I Can't Stick To My Diet.

It's not about maintaining a diet. Diets don't work for a prolonged period of time. You need to change your eating habits. Eating right should be a way of life. In our opinion health should be one of your three priorities. That means eating right, consistently exercising and maintaining the proper body weight.

If health does make it to your list of priorities then eating right becomes part of your daily routine. Health is one of our three priorities so we plan our meals and our exercise routines carefully. If it's not one of your priorities you WILL always struggle to maintain the proper weight.

Playing The Mind Game

We always imagine what we would look like if we didn't eat right. When you are tempted to eat something that's not healthy remember how terrible you always feel afterwards. Your mind knows what's best for your body. You've just chosen to ignore it. So next time you eat that super-sized double cheeseburger meal you better check that mental snapshot. That picture needs to be one of your priorities. Focus on that mental picture and remember that you really are what you eat!

11. I Can't Motivate Myself to Consistently Exercise.

"I need a personal trainer to push me every day". Harris says, "During my travels around the world I visit dozens of new gyms each year. It's mind boggling to see the dependency people have on personal trainers. There are so many people out there that will not exercise on their own. The reasons vary from being lazy, lack of drive or expertise, or solely as a status symbol, which is big in Los Angeles where I live."

We're not condemning fitness experts. They need to make a living as well. Unfortunately, they often times feed off these individuals who cannot motivate themselves. Lack of motivation is probably the number one reason people use them. It's sad but true.

If it's your first time exercising and you're not comfortable learning on your own, then we would recommend hiring a fitness consultant or personal trainer for a few weeks. Most of them have the knowledge and expertise to show you the proper routines. It's important that you don't let the training sessions go for more than a month. The sooner you become self-reliant, the better. Motivate yourself instead of being dependent on someone else. Periodic (i.e., quarterly) checkups to gauge progress or lack there of is acceptable only if you feel it's absolutely necessary.

It's worth doing the research if you're serious about achieving results using a trainer. There are websites that offer free personal trainer online locators that list pre-screened trainers for all 50 states. Look into it. We'd prefer you disciplined yourself, but then again, once you have the knowledge and expertise you can't use that excuse anymore. If this is what's necessary for you to get on this goal, then go for it.

If exercise is going to be part of your daily routine, then it has to be included in your plan as a priority with specific goals and objectives. Once health and fitness become a priority and you've learned the routine ask yourself the following question: Why would I waste my hard earned money on a trainer and be dependent on this individual indefinitely? After all, don't I have something more important to spend my money on?

As most of you fitness freaks already know, it's extremely hard to exercise consistently. Some days it's a real struggle and it's easy to find excuses.

There's always time to exercise as depicted in Table XX. This is an excuse that is affecting your health and quality of life. Here are some other excuses:

> *I'm too busy*
> *I'll do it tomorrow*
> *When I was younger I was very consistent*
> *Before I got married I used to be in great shape*
> *I don't know the routine - I don't know where to begin...*

We put this excuse last for a reason. Whether you're the CEO of a busy household or a corporation, there's always time to exercise. Make the time.

Playing The Mind Game

Harris says, "I played some mind games as I was training my mind to overcome some of those weak moments we all have. These are the actual phrases I used:

> ➢ *If I don't exercise today I'll look like millions of other overweight Americans.*
> ➢ *If I don't exercise today I'll look like shit the rest of my life.*
> ➢ *If I don't exercise today I'll become lazy and complacent.*

These mind games seem crazy but they were mighty effective. I started using some of these in my teens and the rest of them in my twenties. Now I'm 48 years old and I no longer need them. Exercise has become a way of life and I couldn't imagine my life without it."

12. There Have Been So Many Stressful Events in My Life That I Couldn't Handle Anything More Right Now.

Karen writes: The first thing you have to realize is that everyone has a totally different view of what constitutes a stressful event. Our favorite definition of stress is: The confusion created when one's mind overrides the body's basic desire to choke the living shit out of some asshole who desperately needs it. But there are many stressors in our lives beyond other people.

Someone who would make an excuse like the one above is one who prefers to draw attention to the fact that they have a lot to deal with, let stress control them or make a habit of feeling sorry for themselves. We all get ample scares at times in our lives that make us realize we are mortal. Be it car accidents, medical problems or whenever we feel that instant feeling of helplessness over our situation. How do you deal with those times? We refuse to feel sorry for ourselves no matter what the circumstances. Everyone has problems on some level in their lives, but it doesn't mean everyone you meet should hear about them. And it certainly doesn't mean you should stop taking on challenges because of some setbacks that you couldn't control.

Playing The Mind Game

I have never felt others should spend their time worrying about me. That's my job. I tend to deal with things and then if I can help someone else by sharing my experience afterwards I will happily do so. Otherwise, those who enjoy focusing on the negatives will continue to shine a spotlight on things that are now ancient history to me. I have better things to do with my time and I'm sure they do to.

A recent example, and I've had a few in my life, was last year when I started having constant migraine headaches. When the high daily doses of Tylenol and Motrin didn't help I spent a lot of time having medical tests, Magnetic Resonance Imaging (MRI)'s and frustrating appointments with various doctors who were just as perplexed as I was. With every test the results were the same, "The bad news is that you had to endure this torture. The good news; your test is negative."

Harris had asked me to commit to doing this book as this battery of tests had just begun. I had no idea what the outcome of these tests would be but I knew focusing my energy on a new challenge was exactly what I needed. I was prescribed some very strong medication for pain management that made me sleep. Since I didn't tell Harris what I was going through it made for some interesting explanations on my sleep schedule and spontaneous napping!

As you would expect I spent a lot of waiting room time working on this book as a result. As I sat waiting to be seen by a Neurosurgeon to review the images of my brain (and yes it is as freakish as it sounds) I was nervous but again thankful as I looked around the waiting room to see others who had problems much worse than mine.

I had no choice but to stay on pain medication for months until the migraines subsided. Otherwise, it's medical history and everything came out fine. I couldn't imagine how miserable I would have been if I had chosen to focus on my medical issue for 7 months instead of taking the opportunity to write this book! But I know a lot of others who would've chosen that option.

Don't allow your current problems to spoil your future plans. The best thing to alleviate stress is to stay busy and never waste time feeling sorry for yourself or expect others to feel sorry for you. Be thankful, because there are lots of people who have a more stressful life than yours. Just look around you, it doesn't take a brain surgeon to figure that one out.

Being Redundant

It's like participating in any sport, the more you practice the better player you become. Playing mind games is the game plan that gets you to win every game you're in until your mind takes the ball and runs with it.

Harris says, "My mind was in complete control of everything I did. And I do mean <u>everything</u>. My daily routine was orchestrated by my mind. It was that drill sergeant implanted in my head. If I even thought about being lazy maybe just to sleep in on a Saturday morning, it had other plans. It treated all days equally, which meant getting up very early and getting my butt into the gym. Use the mind games to avoid obstacles and manage your routine."

Mind Over Matter

This is what it's all about. Karen says, "My late father-in-law used to say, 'If you put your mind to it, you can do anything.' This phrase is inscribed on the class ring he proudly gave his son upon graduating from the Air Force Academy. Those words had been permanently driven into my husband's mind throughout his childhood. He couldn't appreciate the impact and true meaning of that repetitious statement until that day. The ring is nice, but the mind etching compliments of Dad -- priceless!"

Beautiful Minds

You hear these stories on the news all the time. They are told because they are truly extraordinary. A hiker gets lost in the dead of winter for several days and survives despite the odds. How about all those patients who are given a devastating prognosis and prove dozens of doctors wrong by beating the odds, i.e., walking again or longevity way beyond expectations? There is no doubt that the mind is capable of accomplishing miraculous things. This is even more phenomenal when the mind and body are dependent on each other to complete difficult goals.

Trained minds we admire

Karen says, "I've been fortunate enough to live where a couple of the Olympic Training Centers are located. Training for winter sports are done in Colorado Springs, Colorado at 7,000 feet elevation. Summer sports are the focus of the ARCO Olympic Training Center in Chula Vista, California. I can't imagine how anyone could not be inspired by what these athletes have been able to accomplish with their minds instinctively pushing their bodies to excel. Those invited to train at these specialized training centers are there because there is no one left in their state to compete with. This takes them to the next level and affords them the peer competition they need to excel in their sport. Upon returning home they become mentors who elevate their former teammates up to the next level. Everyone wins. Olympic athletes can only push their bodies as far as their minds will let them. It's just one more example of minds being challenged to go further."

Refined Minds

Some members of the military are required to be in top physical condition at all times. It simply comes with the territory. Not only do they endure rigorous physical training just to be accepted, they are expected to maintain that state of readiness. A few examples of these elite forces are Air Force Pararescuemen, Army Special Forces or Navy Seals. The majority of those in training won't even make it through the intense mental conditioning. They are the ones who are broken first. Why? Any drill instructor will repeat this one a thousand times, "I knew they could do it, but they didn't know they could". They have failed to allow their minds to be trained. Time will not be wasted on anyone who refuses to accept discipline. On the other hand, those who endure it all and make it through are trained to use their minds to push their bodies to fitness levels beyond their dreams.

Enormous Mental Fortitude

This is mind training at its peak. It's strength of mind that allows you to endure pain or adversity with courage. Unleashing this power can mean the difference between life and death. This is how ordinary people survive under extreme circumstances. Perfect examples of this are prisoners of war. They are true heroes in every sense of the word. Some have survived extreme mental and physical torture coupled with years of isolation by training their minds to pull them through it.

We are virtually surrounded by so many people who possess beautifully trained minds. Take every opportunity to learn from them. Soak up every ounce of inspiration possible. The common denominator for each and every one of the examples above is a very fine-tuned or well-trained mind.

7. THE TOTAL PACKAGE

"Intelligence without ambition is a bird without wings."
C. Archie Danielson

The Body Too

As you're training the mind it's important to keep the body in tip-top condition. This means eating healthy and consistently exercising. Your mind needs your body in perfect condition as you're attempting to acquire discipline. Once your mind is trained it will push your body like you never thought possible. It will break down any barrier in your path. Your body will never ask for a day off nor will it want a break. Sound familiar? Without your body in the best possible condition you will be adding another obstacle in your road to success. The body and mind have to work as one. This goes a long way to understanding what you are capable of. This is something the majority of the population struggles with. If you can conquer this goal, then you have begun to understand what discipline is and how much of a dramatic impact it can have on your life. We can't stress this enough.

That doesn't mean you exercise one day a week for one week, the second week you do it twice, etc. or the third week you have too many personal issues to address. Consistently exercising means if you commit to 3 days a week then somehow/someway you make it 3 days a week every week of the year – that equates to 156 workouts!

Stay Ahead of The Game

If you've established a goal of exercising three days a week from this day forward train your mind to stay ahead of the game. If you only go three days a week we guarantee you'll miss your goal because there will be times when you get sick or an emergency will come up. Tell yourself over and over again that emergencies will arise and you will miss that goal unless you start going in 4 days a week on those times of the month when you have a bit more time on your hands. It's like putting money in a savings account just in case you unexpectedly get laid off from work. The return on this investment is feeling healthy everyday.

Push Your Body - It Can Take It

When it comes to our bodies, society has turned us into wimps by telling us:

> ➤ *Don't over exert yourself exercising*
> ➤ *Just take these pills to calm your nerves or take this medication for stress relief*
> ➤ *Get plenty of rest every night, etc.,*

In our opinion listening to so-called medical experts who rarely exercise - if they ever do is a bunch of hogwash. To excel in anything you need to be constantly challenging and pushing yourself. The same goes for your body. Great athletes always push their bodies past any and all barriers. Others who make this a goal can do the same with their body.

Harris writes: I've trained my mind to allow my body to break down all barriers and excel beyond all limitations. Once again it's a game I play each and everyday of my life. The game is quite entertaining. I play a form of Russian roulette with my body (No, not the kind with guns and bullets) using phrases. My favorite phrase while I'm exercising is "I can't be broken". As I exercise 7 days a week I try to outperform yesterday's routine. Over and over again - "I

113

can't be broken". To me challenging oneself is always more exciting and rewarding than status quo.

I exercise extremely hard, even at the age of 48. As a matter of fact although I've exercised consistently since I was 13 I am working out twice as hard now as I enter the second half of my life. Will I be able to keep up this pace in another 30 years – I sincerely doubt it, but my mind will keep trying to push me.

People will ask me why I don't ease up a bit and go into maintenance mode so as not to exert myself. They say that I can still exercise my customary 7 days a week but why not ease up on the old body a bit? To me it's like putting my body into a casket and nailing it shut. My mind has taken over my body and pushes me to improve. Don't baby your body - instead take care of it by eating right and consistently exercise to excel. The stronger you are physically the more mentally tough you will be to conquer all your goals.

Make Exercise Fun

Harris writes: Exercise doesn't have to be unpleasant, yet so many people look upon it as a necessary evil with nothing but sweat and unnecessary pain. There are many other things that people would rather be doing. The number one thing on that list is doing nothing. If you start taking on the challenge of exercising consistently and you bring along a negative attitude then your new goal will be dead in its tracks after a few weeks.

First of all you have to train the mind that exercise is not a supplement to life, it's an integral part of your life. The sooner you can incorporate it into your daily routine - not 3 days a week, or 4 days a week but being able to do some form of exercise every day then you will overcome these barriers. Our bodies need some form of exercise on a regular basis and you don't have to go to the gym each day. You have all kinds of options:

> *Clean house/apartment once a week at a fast pace*
> *Wash/wax your own car*
> *Take long brisk walks to the store, etc.,*

Train your mind that cleaning the house is exercise, as is washing and waxing the car. It really works. You'll get a pretty good sweat out of it and accomplish two things at one time.

As you begin your new fitness routine start with a very positive attitude. Always be upbeat and positive. Even though there will be some bumpy spots on the road with loads of excuses why you shouldn't go, i.e., you're tired, you're feeling sick, you've got too much work to do, etc., you need to go anyway! Push yourself and eventually the mind will take over and automatically push you. (Refer back to the section on Playing Mind Games)

We all know the benefits of exercising regularly:

> ➢ **Reducing stress**
> ➢ **Better conditioning**
> ➢ **Physical well-being**
> ➢ **Mentally up-lifting, etc.,**

So, why are people still getting turned off to exercise? There are many reasons but one of the most common is they're doing the same old routine and getting themselves into a rut. Enthusiasts typically join their local health club (by paying a hefty initiation fee upfront) – all gung-ho to start their new routine. In two weeks they're bored and that's the last you'll see of them. That's how health clubs prosper.

Always change your routine. I never do the same routine 2 weeks in a row (even after 25+ years). For example Table 7.1 outlines below what my typical weekly exercise routine would look like. I happen to enjoy exercising with weights (W) and different types of cardiovascular (C) exercises. On most days I'll normally do 10 minutes of some type of cardiovascular warm-up exercise before I start my weights.

Table 7.1: Typical weekly exercises routine

	Week 1	Week2
Monday	Warm-up **W**-Arms (1.5 -hours) **C**- riding stationery bike (30 minutes)	**C**-Precor/EFX machine (1 hour) Abdominal exercises (30 minutes)
Tuesday	Warm-up **W**-Legs (1.5 hours) **C**-riding stationery bike (30 minutes)	Warm-up **W**-Chest and Arms for 2 hours
Wednesday	Warm-up **W**-Shoulders & back (1.5 hours) Abdominal exercises (30 minutes)	Warm-up **W**-Legs (1.5 hours) **C**-riding stationery bike (30 minutes)
Thursday	Warm-up **W**-Chest (1 hour) **C**-running/walking on tread mill/street (30 minutes)	**W**-Shoulders & back (1.5 hours) Abdominal exercises (20 minutes)
Friday	Warm-up Abdominal exercises (20 minutes) **W**-arms (1.5 hours) **C**-Precor/EFX machine (30 minutes)	Warm-up **W**-Arms (1.5 -hours) and **C**-riding stationery bike (30 minutes)
Saturday	Warm-up **W**-Legs (1.5 hours) **C**-riding stationery bike (30 minutes)	Warm-up **W**-Chest (45 minutes) Take a bike ride in the afternoon for at least an hour.
Sunday	**W**-Shoulders & back (1.5 hours) Abdominal exercises (20 minutes)	Warm-up **W**-Legs (1.5 hours) Do a 30-90 minute walk or hike.

People will occasionally tell me to take a day off from exercise saying, "Hey, it's healthier for you to occasionally rest your body". This is one of the most frequent comments I hear. My reply is always the same. "Yes I agree to an extent, it's a good idea to occasionally take a week off but I can't do it. My mind is so well programmed that it pushes my body to exercise everyday of the year." If I change my routine everyday then the particular parts I exercised on Monday would get a few days rest before hitting them again. The body only needs 24-48 hours to rest a particular muscle group (i.e., chest, legs, arms, etc.) to rebuild damaged muscle cells.

Karen says, "If you don't want to frequent a health club its worth the investment to buy a treadmill, or whatever works for you. Time saved commuting to the gym is gained and you can catch up on the morning or evening news at the same time. You have no excuses not to make it happen on a regular basis. I was always at work and missed one of my favorite shows, Oprah, so I recorded it and always watched the tape during my workout. I didn't allow myself to watch it unless I was working out. Record your favorite songs like the aerobic instructors do and use that if it gets you going. Exercising indoors can be something you look forward to. Really. The payoff is enormous."

Eating Smart

The English language should abolish the word diet. We hate it with a passion. Unfortunately, there are so many books written with the word diet as the subject matter it has brainwashed much of the population. Eating smart has nothing to do with dieting – diets rarely work. It's all about training the mind to eat properly and consistently. You don't have to read a "diet" book to figure this stuff out.

What to Eat and When

You simply need to change your eating habits. It's all about strict maintenance of your carbohydrate intake as well as portion control. Eat the bulk of your carbohydrates in the morning and at lunch. If you feel the urge to eat some carbohydrates in the evening only do it occasionally - for instance once a week and keep the portions very small.

We know what you're thinking. Where do desserts fit into this plan? Once you've got your mind and body used to this way of eating you'll be able to indulge in sweets once in a while and preferably at lunch (since they are carbohydrates) but don't make a habit of it. The less you submit to them the better off you'll be. The longer the time between eating desserts the better since you'll just crave them less if you don't indulge in them quite as often. Once a week if you must, but don't forget; the harder you are working on your daily workouts the less you will crave the things that are obstacles to achieving your physical goal. Eating properly is about having control. Once you've acquired discipline then you may allow yourself to indulge on occasion because you have a plan to control it.

Table 7.2 below provides you with an example of what to eat if you exercise regularly (minimum 3 days a week) in the morning. For the best results eat 5 meals a day.

Table 7.2: Typical meal

Time	Type of Meal	Description of Meal
5:00 a.m. **(Wake up)**	Small snack - eat some sort of carbohydrate and protein before you exercise.	Combination or separate items: banana, low fat yogurt, toast, bagel, etc., It's OK to put a little jelly, or low fat cream cheese on your toast before you exercise (make sure you give your stomach at least 45 minutes to thoroughly digest your meal before exercising).
7:00 a.m.	Breakfast – Eat a good size breakfast after you exercise. OK to eat a fair amount of carbohydrates but need to include plenty of protein.	Combination or separate items: Eggs, toast, fruits, milk, low fat yogurt, cereal or oatmeal.
10:00 a.m.	Mid morning snack with small amounts of carbohydrates and some type of protein.	Combination or separate items: Protein bar or drink, low fat yogurt, perhaps some low fat cheese or a little bit of fruit.
12:30 p.m.	Lunch – lean protein and carbohydrates in moderation.	Combination or separate items: Turkey or chicken sandwich, fish, vegetables or salad.
3:30 p.m.	Small afternoon snack – decrease amounts of carbohydrates but keep up the protein.	Combination or separate items: Protein bar or drink, low fat yogurt, tuna fish, etc.
6:30 p.m.	Very little to no carbohydrates keep up the protein but decrease the overall amount of your meal.	Fish, chicken, lean beef, and perhaps occasionally a small salad.
Evening	No snacks – if you're starving have some type of protein (one with very low carbohydrates). No other munchies.	

Proteins consist of but are not limited to:

> **Eggs, lean meats, fish, yogurt, milk, cheese, protein drinks/bars, etc.**

Carbohydrates consist of but are not limited to:

> **Breads, potatoes, rice, pasta, vegetables, fruits, etc.**

If you exercise in the evening follow the same plan but you can have carbohydrates before you exercise. The same rules apply after your workout though, meaning very little to no carbohydrates after your workout and for the rest of the evening.

Values

Values are guiding principles. They are basic beliefs that are the fundamental assumptions upon which all subsequent actions are based. As a whole, values define the personality and character of an individual. Values are the essence of an individual and provide guidelines by which to make consistent decisions. In reality, values are ideals that are indicative of one's vision of how the world should work. To be successful one must adhere to personal and professional values.

Acquiring discipline means being that extraordinary person who will go out of their way to help people. It means being honest, sincere and a caring individual at all times. It also means doing what is right, regardless of any sort of personal sacrifices.

Professional value means not backstabbing people at work. Politics run rampant throughout all organizations, and many employees have a bad habit of getting their co-workers in trouble for the sake of improving their professional careers. Climbing the management ladder is exciting; with each new promotion comes a completely new set of challenges and opportunities. It's not that difficult to walk all over people, and doing so sometimes comes with financial rewards. We feel its much more important to be respected by everyone around us than to selfishly compromise our values and destroy the reputation of others to satisfy our own means. Acquire discipline, and you need never bring yourself down to this level. Below are some examples:

➤ Loyalty given/loyalty returned

Be loyal to your friends, colleagues, and family. By this we mean being dedicated, considerate, and willing to make sacrifices.

➤ No surprises

Never surprise your friends, colleagues, or associates. Difference of opinion should be worked out prior to any public meetings. It is your responsibility to make sure no one is surprised – surprises lead to lack of trust, confusion, and arguments.

➤ Mutual Respect

Respect must be earned and cannot be assumed. Never embarrass anyone. Not only is it disrespectful but it ruins relationships and trust. Also never make a commitment unless you can fulfill your obligation. It's very easy to lose respect for someone when they never fulfill their commitment. Treat others as you would like to be treated.

➤ Honesty and candor

It is surprisingly easy to be honest and totally lacking in candor. If you need to be asked the precise question to elicit the required information then you are not doing your job. It is not enough to be honest in everything you say and do but, without being brutally frank, it is important to understand what is being asked and to answer with candor. Don't hoard information and don't spin information. Be objective and make sure what you say is supportable.

➤ Integrity

"A person is not given integrity. It results from the relentless pursuit of honesty at all times."
Anonymous

121

Your word is absolutely and unwaveringly reliable. What you see and hear is what you get. Walk the talk. It's painfully obvious when someone conducts their lives in a negative way, but claims to do the exact opposite when in the company of others. Better to admit to yourself that you need to change than to try to convince yourself and others that "things are better than they appear". You will gain respect by being honest about your shortcomings and your integrity will be intact.

> "Integrity is what we do, what we say, and what
> we say we do."
> *Don Galer*

➤ **Professionalism**

This encompasses all of the following; being objective, knowledgeable, competent, dependable, reliable, thorough, disciplined, and well mannered.

Learn from Others

> "What you dislike in another take care to correct
> in yourself."
> *Thomas Sprat*

Learn, learn, and continue to learn from others. Whether the individual has negative qualities or an individual has positive mannerisms, apply it to your life. Harris says, "I've learned academic qualities from many brilliant and politically savvy individuals. It was like going to college and taking courses but instead I received real life on the job training. I've also watched and studied the most disruptive and belligerent individuals." It's important to keep an open mind and learn from as many individuals as you possibly can. It will only help you become a better human being.

Only the Strong Will Survive

We all know this to be true. Being disciplined has everything to do with being strong. You will learn to build your mental and physical strength and that alone will ensure your survival under any circumstances. You will persevere no matter what comes your way. When you're dealt a significant setback you will be like a cat and always land on your feet without fail. You will have unshakeable confidence because you won't ever have to worry about your livelihood. Knowing you are as strong as you can be goes a long way to building your confidence and that is why survival of the fittest is a fact of life. Strength builds confidence. If you aren't at your peak, then you might be able to leap tall buildings, but if your confidence is questionable then you may need to pack a parachute. And it may not be in a single-bound; more like a few running jumps on some medium-sized buildings for practice. In other words, you may not survive the jump at all. Why risk it?

8.   IT'S NEVER ENOUGH

> "Whenever an individual or a business decides that success has been attained, progress stops."
> *Thomas J. Watson*

Now that you have accomplished so many goals and objectives in life – isn't it enough? No – it's <u>NEVER</u> enough. With discipline you will never have accomplished enough. There will always be new goals to conquer. Your mind will be so well trained - try and turn it off for a while. Try and tell yourself that you now have dozens of major accomplishments under your belt and maybe it's time to take it easy or maybe it's time for retirement. Go ahead and try! Harris says, "Retirement is a 4-letter word to me. I could have retired at the age of 40 but the thought of waking up each day without goals and objectives and just playing golf, going fishing, and being on a permanent vacation… that novelty will last about a month. Is that what life's all about? People go on vacation for rest and relaxation to de-stress and re-group-that's fine and I'm all for that but doing it everyday for the rest of your life? I'm breaking out in a sweat at the thought of it! When you acquire discipline forget it – your mind is in one mode for the rest of your life. Regardless of how many accomplishments you have <u>they will NEVER be enough!</u>"

The Continuous Thirst For Knowledge

> "It is best to learn as we go, not go as we have learned".
> *Leslie Jeanne Sahler*

One of the biggest thrills in life is to learn and to keep learning. For us, if we stop learning and experiencing new challenges then you might as well stick a fork in us 'cause we're done. With discipline you always want to learn more. We're not talking about just formal education that you get by going to school. That is highly recommended and a given these days, but that is only the beginning. We're talking about after high school and college and beyond. We mean those everyday experiences and challenges we all face. Whether it comes from traveling (cultures, languages, etc.), understanding your body's physical limitations, or completing a huge project at work; keep on learning. With discipline the thirst for knowledge will never be quenched.

Patience

> "Our real Blessings often Appear to us In the Shapes of pains, losses and disappointments; but let us have Patience, and we soon shall see them in their Proper Figures."
> *Joseph Addison*

Patience is a difficult trait to acquire because when you're disciplined you feel like you can conquer the world and nothing should slow you down. Unfortunately, when you acquire discipline it will be almost impossible to be patient. Your mind and body are going at one speed; pedal to the metal every minute of the day. Do we have a solution for you? If we did we'd use it on ourselves, because we, like everyone else know how important patience is. We have to work at it and remind ourselves all the time and still it doesn't stick with us. This is the only attribute that we've had a hard time training the mind for – oh well, we'll take all the other benefits with discipline anytime. Our perseverance will continue to try and gain patience whether we like it or not and we know someday we will possess it.

It's Much More Than Being A Leader

> "The most important quality in a leader is that of being acknowledged as such. All leaders whose fitness is questioned are clearly lacking in force."
> *Andre Maurois*

Once you realize that you are being looked upon as a leader, either by appointed title or by being put on a pedestal by others its time to take your position seriously. With leadership comes responsibility. "Do as I say and not as I do" won't fly. Leading by example is what separates the true leaders from the ones who are leaders merely on paper or by given job title. If you respect yourself, or have discipline, then others will respect you. We've all worked for leaders who we don't respect and those are times we must remember – no matter how unpleasant – because remembering a bad leader serves as a reminder of what we never want to become. Use that experience to keep yourself on track to be a much better leader by learning from their mistakes. Actions do speak louder than words.

So why does it matter if our leaders are physically fit? The downfall of many a leader is that Achilles heel or weakness that was insignificant until their leadership role became official. Anyone who is elected as a leader and is in the public eye has to consider how they might be perceived. People can relate to a fluctuating waistline, but that alone shows weakness. So what if a role model prefers fast food to workouts? Unfortunately in most cases, one weakness leads to another. Before long there isn't much left to respect and suddenly people begin to question everything they thought their leader stood for. In reality, our belief in one's leadership abilities is of utmost importance. If they are struggling to manage themselves, then how can we expect them to manage others successfully? It all matters because image is everything. Who wants to follow and support a weak leader?

As a leader, you set the pace for those who support you. Karen says, "I've worked for 15 different bosses in the past 18 years because of our nomadic military lifestyle. I've also supervised others. That means if I work in one place for 3 years on a military base, I will see a turnover of 2-3 bosses because they are also being shuffled around. The hardest working leaders make the best bosses, hands down. When you know they are doing their best to shake things up and get the job done, then you will be motivated to go the extra mile to support them in each and every endeavor. There's nothing more rewarding than working hard for a common goal."

If you continuously take yourself to new levels of accomplishments others will want to emulate the discipline that drives you to new heights like a runaway freight train. You must discipline yourself first to be the best person you can be so others take you seriously. Leaders who lead themselves are destined to become leaders of others. Leaders who fail to lead themselves will quickly lose favor and be labeled forever.

"Nothing so conclusively proves a man's ability to lead others as what he does from day to day to lead himself."
Thomas J. Watson

Masters of Mental Stimulation

So what are extraordinary leaders like in real life? Generally, they are harder on themselves than anyone else could ever be. They go on about the business of leading themselves as well as others and continue to set the standards in both these challenging roles. The following is a CBS News 60 Minutes II interview with Charlie Rose. It describes what true leaders possess. It's selflessly giving their heart and soul towards mentoring others to achieve common goals. Remember the mind and body connection we mentioned earlier; it's vital to spark the flame of discipline, which is really just mental stimulation with the switch stuck in the "on" position.

His name is Mike Krzyzewski, and he is the head basketball coach at Charlie Rose's alma mater, Duke University in North Carolina. "Coach K," as he's known, has put his teams near the top of the NCAA basketball tournament nine times in the last 16 years - three times as champion. And he has done it with a style unlike anything you would expect.

He doesn't talk like a typical coach, or act like one. Though he can be tough, and temperamental, Krzyzewski is hardly a tyrant. He hugs, he listens, he supports. He wants every player at every game to feel he has something at stake.

Says Krzyzewski: "You have a chance for everybody to have ownership. That's the ultimate goal. You know, where the team is owned by everybody on that team... It's always we."

He says that psychology is the most important aspect of his success: "I think it's the most important factor. What happens in sport a lot is that - and it happens in business too. People try to learn the business or they learn the sport

127

- they learn the X's and O's and all that. And the time they spend on that is so disproportional with the time they spend learning about people. There has to be a combination there. There has to be an excessive amount of time just being spent with people. These are the people who make the X's and O's work."

Krzyzewski's emphasis on "we" - on teamwork -- extends in every direction, including the Duke student body. This makeshift village outside Cameron Indoor Stadium is called K-Ville. Before big home games, students camp out for weeks for their chance to get tickets. They're called the "Cameron Crazies."

The reason they're doing it is because they're part of the team, we win and we lose together," says Krzyzewski. "In other words, whenever we play Maryland or Wake Forest or North Carolina or whoever, it's not just the Duke basketball team on the court; it's all of us. They're not just part of the team, they're passionately part. You know one of the rules in there is that you stand for every second of every game. You want to stand the entire game."

That kind of devotion and enthusiasm has made Krzyzewski not only a winning basketball coach, but one of the most sought after speakers in the country. Companies hire him to fire up employees. His approach is thoughtful, almost fatherly.

In the huddle, he will tell each of his players that they are good. "There hasn't been a player that I've coached that at some times doesn't need to be told, 'You're the best guy right now.' We all feel insecure at times. And a lot of times, the guy who's the leader, or the top player, can be the loneliest player on the team because the other guys on the team don't think he needs anything. But the lead guy needs stuff, too, otherwise, he gets drained."

That kind of sensitivity is surprising when you consider the man who was Krzyzewski's mentor: Bobby Knight - the controversial but successful coach who recruited Krzyzewski to play for him at West Point, and later assist him at Indiana. Krzyzewski learned a lot of skills from Knight. But chair-throwing, evidently, wasn't one of them.

One example of the Coach K method: In last year's NCAA tournament, the Blue Devils got to the championship without one of their star players, Carlos Boozer, who had been sidelined with an injury. Boozer's replacement, Casey Sanders, had played well. But at half time of the final, the game was close and Carlos Boozer was ready to play. With the championship on the line, here's how the master of motivation handled it.

At halftime, Krzyzewski made sure that both Sanders and Boozer were comfortable with the fact that Boozer would start the second half. That's probably not how Bobby Knight would have done it. But it worked for Krzyzewski - Duke won.

Krzyzewski grew up in Chicago, the son of an elevator operator and a cleaning woman.

Coach K: "My mom was the happiest person alive. And for her whole life, she had two dresses in her closet. She didn't take any money with her. You know what I mean? It's not about what you accumulate, it's about what you do."

What he wanted to do was teach. Basketball was his way to do it. When he came to Duke in 1981, he was 32. Both the Duke alumni and the local press were skeptical. There were lots of questions about this Krzyzewski. Five hundred wins later, they named the court after him.

Charlie Rose: What does this mean to you, Coach K Court?
Coach K: "Well, the main thing it means is that I have a long name and they couldn't get the whole name on there or that a basketball court is too small."

To make it on Coach K's court takes a special kind of player. Recruiting those players is the first part of Krzyzewski's method - and he isn't just looking for basketball skills.

"First of all, I choose people who have already understood looking up to authority," he says. "They've had some authority in their life. You know, good parents, good teachers."

But to be in the family, there's a price. Nobody knows that better than his wife, Mickie: "He wants something back. He wants the investment from those people that he's putting in, he says I will give you 100 percent, how much will you give me? And it better be 100 percent. Or you break his heart. He's not gonna yell at you, not gonna kick you off the team. He's not gonna berate you in public, do anything like that. But he's gonna get heartbroken, and the guys can't handle that. They hate when they break his heart."

He takes every loss personally. He may nurture his players. But he's brutal on himself. His wife remembers one loss in particular, earlier this year. She says her husband was looking in the mirror and cussing himself out. He called himself a compromising son of a bitch, she says.

129

Why is he so hard on himself? "I don't have anybody coaching me. I have to coach me. I mean I have to be the most realistic with myself. I have to be the most self-critical."

Now 54, Krzyzewski recently signed a lifetime contract to stay at Duke. He says he's happiest here in North Carolina, finding ways to inspire his team. Motivating them is what motivates him.

"I love the kids that we bring into our program. And basically, because I feel like they're part of our family."

Disciplined

"The man who views the world at 50 the same as he did at 20 has wasted 30 years of his life."
Muhammad Ali

Don't let your life pass you by. Follow your PRIME and train the mind and success will come your way. Discipline is the catalyst to that success. Whether it's excelling in your career, providing more quality time with your family, or consistently exercising without a trainer, discipline is the key to helping you achieve your accomplishments.

Benefits

Below are the attributes you will obtain with discipline:

➢ <u>Accomplishment after accomplishment:</u>

Ability to accomplish more than you ever thought possible. Not only will you be able to accomplish all your goals, you will never be satisfied with what you've already accomplished. The hunger and drive to accomplish more will stay with you for the rest of your life.

➢ **Drive**:

You'll know how to motivate yourself everyday of the year. Your mind will do it for you – ALWAYS. We actually have a very hard time relaxing or sleeping because our minds are always pushing us to go, go, go! Once you train the mind you'll never be complacent again.

➢ **Perseverance**:

> "I think that if I keep working at this and want it
> badly I can have it."
> *Lee J. Iacocca*

You'll never give up on accomplishing your goals. You will have some obstacles and barriers along the way but you will do whatever it takes to avoid those obstacles and break down those barriers. You will never give up until you accomplish your goal. We cannot overemphasize how important it is to stay focused on your goals. As we experience many challenges and distractions in our lives, it becomes easy to falter. Harris says, "Many times during my quest for Discipline, giving up was the ticket to social acceptance especially in my pressure-packed teenage years. However, I remained focused on my goals, knowing what my priorities and goals stood for in the long haul."

Remaining focused on your goals will help you to prosper in so many ways. There will be days when those outlandish and crazy goals are too much of a burden. Staying in bed and forgetting about everything is the easy way out. Never give up! It may sound like an old cliché, but you should do as all athletes do when the going gets tough: they dig down for a little something extra to accomplish those goals.

➢ **Values**:

You will believe, honor, and practice values i.e., sincerity, integrity, honesty, loyalty, respect, etc. You will be respected and admired by your friends, colleagues, and peers. What's really cool is when people who don't even know you personally will speak highly of you. This is when you know you've got it. Your advice will be solicited on all kinds of topics and you will find yourself mentoring people just about all the time. There is nothing more rewarding than being recognized for your values.

> ## **Persistence and Determination**

> "Nothing in this world can take the place of persistence. Talent will not; nothing is more common than unsuccessful people with talent. Genius will not; unrewarded genius is almost a proverb. Education will not; the world is full of educated derelicts. Persistence and determination alone are omnipotent."
> *Calvin Coolidge*

There's really nothing else we can add except that with discipline you will <u>never</u> give up on any of your present or future endeavors. Quitting will not be in your vocabulary. You will find whatever means to resolve an obstacle. With discipline you will become a wiser person. We always like to say that a clever person solves a problem, and a wise person avoids it.

> "People of mediocre ability sometimes achieve outstanding success because they don't know when to quit. Most men succeed because they are determined to."
> *George Allen*

The formal definition of determination is: *having one's mind made up, decided; resolved*. With discipline comes determination they go hand in hand. Make up your mind once and for all. This goes back to training the mind. No one can stop you, except yourself, if you are not determined.

Karen writes: If you haven't had the pleasure of having your household goods and vehicle shipped overseas to a remote assignment then you can't fully appreciate this story. For me, it's an experience I won't soon forget. The good news is that you are allowed to bring one vehicle to Iceland - the bad news is that ships are slow and you won't have it for several weeks. So we used the Icelandic base taxi if we were up for a rally racing adventure or you risk your own life by walking in inclement weather that goes from bad to very bad most of the time. The base bus is an option, but with all the stops it makes you can walk to just about anywhere you need to go much faster and if you're lucky you'll have a 50-knot wind to get you there even faster than that crazy taxi option.

I didn't want to waste time waiting for our vehicle to arrive, since I knew my husband and I would have to share it anyway and I don't like to rely on others for anything, including transportation. So I decided to begin my search for employment thinking I would have all my work clothes and a vehicle long before a job would become available on the base because everyone said jobs were hard to come by. I would have ample time to get us settled. Yeah, right.

A part-time position opened up at the school and our apartment was across the street from it. I wanted full-time, but I decided to get into the civil service system as soon as possible and planned on advancing later. I knew that everyone would want this job because it was from 10-2, making it perfect for Moms who had kids in school. We were dinks (dual income, no kids) then. The day the position posted was a "white out" day. That's what you get when you combine heavy snow with high winds, which causes questionable visibility. Alerts were on the base channel telling everyone to use the buddy system when going out, make sure your parkas were donned with the usual reflectors and stay where you are. Yeah, right.

The Civilian Personnel Office (CPO) was down the street a bit. I bundled up, called my husband and told him I was going to get a job today if it killed me. With the wind pushing me it was a struggle not to fall over - again. Even with the parka hood that extends like a periscope about 6" from my face I was still soaking wet from the horizontal snow blasting me the entire time. I didn't realize how crazy this idea was until I blew through the CPO door and was met with looks of disbelief by a room of Icelanders who were standing around chatting about the storm. I pulled off my hood and my hair was wet like I just got out of the shower. I handed them my application and said, "This job is perfect for me right now and not only am I qualified to fill it, I'm willing to go the extra mile everyday, not just in white out conditions." They gave me some hot chocolate and kept me around long enough so everyone had a chance to get a glimpse of the crazy American chick. I took advantage of it because I knew they would all remember my name and my determination would carry me onto other jobs, and it did. I worked at 3 different jobs in the 2.5 years I was there and they were all very cool in their own way. I loved them all and each one was a step further ahead.

Determination also got me home, but at times I had serious doubts. Going against the wind was brutal. I was content just staying vertical, but it took every ounce of strength and leaning forward with all my might to take each step. At times I couldn't see the buildings that I knew were right next to me. I stopped at each one along the way and rested. It was so exhausting and my throat was raw from the wind blasting down it as I was breathing heavily to make any progress at all. I stopped at the hot dog stand and wished I had brought money because a lamb dog was sounding like an excellent last meal at that point.

I know what you're thinking, why didn't you just call for a Taxi or someone to come and get you? I'm not built that way. I love a challenge and this was one I had to take because I knew I could do this. I was so thrilled to reach the door of our apartment building but I was exhausted. I must've stood there for an entire minute with my hand within inches of the doorknob battling the wind to reach it. It was a surreal experience that I thought only happened to adventure seekers. Hmmm, maybe I should've just taken the bus. Yeah, right.

When I got home 30 very long minutes later there was a message on my machine. I got the job. I know my experience alone would've gotten me that job. Being able to impress Icelanders who are some of the most hard-working, determined and resilient people that I've ever met was priceless.

> "Studies indicate that the one quality all successful people have is persistence. They're willing to spend more time accomplishing a task and to persevere in the face of many difficult odds. There's a very positive relationship between people's ability to accomplish a task and the time they're willing to spend on it."
> *Dr.Joyce (Diane Bauer) Brothers*

➢ **Positive attitude:**

> "Sooner or later, those who win are those who think they can."
> *Dr. Paul Tournier*

Regardless of the situation you will have a positive attitude. Everything will be in your reach. There is nothing you will not be able to conquer. Staying positive will also allow you to heal faster from mental and physical injuries. Being negative is a huge deterrent and will be a thing of the past.

Changing your attitude can change everything. This one is major because it is so powerful. Optimism can be learned. Some people seek professional counseling only to learn that they simply need to change their pessimistic view of things. Approach life with optimism and people will naturally be attracted to you. There is always a bright side if you look hard enough. Sometimes you may have to squint really hard to see it, but its there more often than not! Research shows that people who have a better sense of control tend to be most optimistic. We think pessimists have a distorted view of reality and optimists see things accurately. Decide to be happy and you will be happy - regardless of circumstances working against you. Practice being optimistic as you're training your mind because your happiness depends on it.

➢ **Courage:**

> "We need the iron qualities that go with true manhood. We need the positive virtues of resolution, of courage, of indomitable will, of power to do without shrinking the rough work that must always be done."
> *Theodore Roosevelt*

You'll have the ability to take on challenges that you never dreamt possible whether they're professional or personal. You'll have the courage to take on the world. All these attributes go hand in hand with one another. Once you apply your PRIME to your life you will be utterly amazed at how quickly these qualities will begin stacking up in your favor. You'll be like an unstoppable snowball going downhill picking up speed (and qualities, of course) along the way. Just watch out for the trees (or obstacles) along the way.

➢ **Feeling secure:**

You'll feel secure about everything i.e., relationships, career, financial planning, accomplishing goals, etc. You will be beaming with confidence to take on all challenges. That's the great thing about having discipline, its just like having dignity or any other attribute, no one can take that away from you. You'll go from being a question mark to being a living, breathing exclamation point! You know where you are going and you <u>will</u> get there come hell or high water.

➢ **Confidence:**

> "Confidence, like art, never comes from having all the answers; it comes from being open to all the questions."
> *Earl Gray Stevens*

You'll be oozing with confidence. You will be able to take on any challenge regardless of the degree of difficulty. You will have the will and determination to succeed at anything. You now have confidence to take on the world. You can accomplish whatever you desire. Nothing can stop you from completing those goals – absolutely nothing. This newfound confidence is not cockiness. Your mind is so well trained it knows what it can do and it also knows what its limitations are. Your mind will not let your head swell. If you let that happen then you'd have to widen all the doors in your house to fit your inflated head through them. We don't want to waste our time or money on renovations that could be avoided. Heed the warning signs.

➢ **Knowledge:**

You'll have a continuous thirst for knowledge. It's that feeling of not ever wanting to stop learning whether it's about a new career, additional education, travel, reading books, or everyday experiences.

Live and learn. You can't have one without the other. Once you stop learning you will immediately stop growing. We all need to keep searching for those things that will make us better. If seeking knowledge were not important for mankind then we'd all be living like Fred and Wilma Flintstone and Barney and Betty Rubble.

➢ **Enthusiasm:**

> "Nothing great was ever achieved without enthusiasm."
> *Ralph Waldo Emerson*

You'll be upbeat and enthusiastic for everything you take on. You'll have it for every aspect of life. To accomplish your many new goals you can't be upbeat one day and down another. Having a true purpose in life lends itself to enthusism. People who are self-absorbed are severely lacking in enthusiasm. Look outside of yourself often to find what's good about the world around you. Then go about making contributions in your corner of the world to make it better. This is another highly addictive attribute.

➤ <u>**Energy**</u>:

Your mind will be your greatest ally giving you the physical energy to keep you strong to take on these many challenges. Your mind and body will become a powerful force, a source of relentless energy. It's the greatest tool you'll possess for the rest of your existence on this planet. When you're running your life as a business you can't help but be energetic. Things will always be happening to keep you going because this is how you function best.

➤ <u>**Happiness**</u>:

> "Happiness does not come from doing easy work but from the afterglow of satisfaction that comes after the achievement of a difficult task that demanded our best."
> *Theodore Isaac Rubin*

It may sound corny but because you're taking full advantage of your life and accomplishing more than ever before you can't help but be happy. We both have been telling people for as long as we can remember that if we died today we would die happy. We have always done what we set out to do, basked in the glory of our accomplishments and lived to tell about it. Life's journey is as fun as reaching the destination. We've done more in our lives than most people twice our age because we began setting and accomplishing goals in our early teens. Every struggle was a life lesson that we cherish. Karen says, "Never having to depend on anyone but myself for my happiness was and always will be important to me. Because I am disciplined happiness is another benefit that comes along with the territory."

137

➢ **Never being satisfied:**

Probably not what most people tell you, is it? Shouldn't this say be satisfied with what you have? No it shouldn't! Once you acquire discipline you will never be satisfied with what you have whether it be career, physical appearance, knowledge, etc. You will always be hungry and we're not talking about your favorite fast food place that advertises relentlessly when you're at your weakest! Staying hungry is the key to success. Always remember - don't settle. Settle for more.

➢ **Being Consistent:**

"The secret of success is consistency of purpose."
Benjamin Disraeli

If you were to ask us to pick one word that describes discipline it's consistency. Being consistent means being energetic and upbeat every day of the week regardless of the situation. In your attempt to acquire discipline you can't be full of energy and up one day and running on empty on other days. There will be those days where you'll have personal issues to deal with as we all do. You may be feeling down for a few hours or even a day or two depending on the situation but being consistent means being able to rebound as quickly as possible and continue your normal routine.

You'll be focused on your priorities and goals every day of the week and having enough energy without drinking 5 cups of coffee a day. Managing your life as if it were a business to acquire discipline truly means being consistent. The secret to excelling in every facet of life (i.e., health, career, family, etc.) is consistency.

Summary

"There are no short cuts to any place worth going."
(Source Unknown)

As you can see from the impressive list above, acquiring discipline will change your life forever but it won't come easy. It will probably take a few years. Will it be worth the years of investment? What do you think? Who wouldn't want all these attributes? An impressive list like this won't be handed to anyone on a silver platter. You'll have to earn it by completing your goals on schedule and your priorities will become a way of life.

The only negative aspect of acquiring discipline is that it will be difficult to relax at times. Your mind and body are in a different mode now – full speed ahead! Will you ever be able to relax again? Sure, but not as frequent and not for a very long period of time. A good example would be watching a major sporting event i.e., the Super Bowl – will you be able to sit around for 3.5 hours – we suppose anything is possible, but ONLY after you've accomplished your priorities for that day.

It's Not About Money

> "Think it more satisfactory to live richly than die rich."
> *Sir Thomas Browne*

Harris writes: I have money but it doesn't excite me and it doesn't fulfill my life. Sure it's nice to have and we all need it but it doesn't make me happy. The feeling is very superficial and hollow, its tangible, but it ends there. It is certainly a way to measure success, but it's the least important in the big picture. It's nothing compared to accomplishing a major goal. <u>What a charge!</u> The feeling is real and will stay with you for the rest of your life. Even at the age of 48 I remember each of my minor and major goals I accomplished in my teens and twenties. Till this day each one of those accomplishments puts a smile on my face. I'm sure you've heard it before and it may sound a bit cliché but <u>money isn't everything</u>. The best things in life are free. However, you must earn a lot of them for yourself.

> "The best things in life aren't things."
> *Art Buchwald*

It's all about **accomplishments!** That's what really turns us on. Why bother living or just plain old existing if you did the same old boring thing every day of your life. With discipline comes enthusiasm for life and the enjoyment of constantly accomplishing. There's no greater feeling in the world than successfully accomplishing that major goal that you've invested years of your life into.

> "Real riches are the riches possessed inside."
> *B.C. Forbes*

Failure Will Not Be In Your Vocabulary

> "You may be disappointed if you fail, but you are doomed if you don't try."
> *Beverly Sills*

Harris says, "I agree with most of the quote above especially that 'you are doomed if you don't try.' The part I don't totally agree with is the first part that suggests 'You shouldn't be disappointed.' If you fail a goal you should be pissed off at yourself - downright irate - not disappointed. You need to be afraid to death of failure. As I was trying to acquire discipline I trained my mind to be so afraid of failure – calling myself every name in the book you can think of in preparation for failure. Yes - in preparation for it because it's inevitable-right? Wrong! You can never tell yourself failure is OK - it's just another one of life's little learning experiences. Although it is you can't tell yourself that – silly as it may sound. The more you **train the mind** that it's the worst possible thing that can happen to you the better your odds will be that you will <u>never</u> fail. I'm very proud to say that I have hundreds of great accomplishments under my belt and I met them without failing even one goal."

9.   RETIREMENT

> "Age is only a number, a cipher for the records.
> A man can't retire his experience. He must use it.
> Experience achieves more with less energy and
> time."
> *Bernard Mannes Baruch*

We can't understand why senior citizens don't rally to replace this word with something more relative to their lives today.   After all, this is a period of your life that you have worked most of your life to reach. Having accomplished all that, it seems rather anticlimactic to aspire to a place called retirement. We've been to retirement ceremonies and always felt a sadness for the person retiring because frankly, they didn't seem all that psyched about the prospect themselves! Society has placed this idea in our heads that we're supposed to slow down considerably as of a predetermined date. It's not the part about leaving our occupation after years of dedicated service that bothers us. It's the whole idea of the word itself and the negative message it conveys. Check out the definitions below and tell us that you're still looking forward to retirement after reading it. Those of you who are officially retired will find that it does not reflect the reality of your lives and will most likely get a chuckle out of them.

Retire: To go to bed. To fall back; retreat. To remove from active service. To take out of circulation.

Retired: Withdrawn from business or public life.

Retirement: A place of seclusion or privacy; retreat

It's downright depressing! Having said that, lets talk about what we hope retirement will hold for us.

Finally, your time is yours to spend as freely as you would like on your own terms. Yeah baby! Senior discounts and early bird dinners are ours for the taking. Pop in those dentures, help me find the car keys and let's go! Time waits for no one and this is never more evident than after one retires. It's pretty amazing that if you ask someone what their plans are for retirement, it becomes clear that they haven't given it much serious thought. This is probably why a lot of seniors will return to work. They have failed to plan for their later years while they were still relatively young. They simply haven't managed their time very well after years of having others monopolize it for them. It's human nature to keep learning, achieving accomplishments and having a true sense of purpose. All these things invoke excitement. It's not that anyone misses the "work" of their careers; they miss the discipline and the challenges that are required of them. They just haven't figured out how to challenge themselves to achieve their own accomplishments. To love life is to have that excitement.

Plan Your Future, Or Others Will Gladly Plan It For You

"Time is the coin of your life. It is the only coin you have, and you can determine how it will be spent. Be careful lest you let other people spend it for you."
Carl Sandburg

Most of us spend the better part of a year just planning for our wedding day. You've got decades to work on your retirement goals. What's that, you haven't had the time? God willing, you've got a few more decades left on earth. It seems the last few decades of your existence is worth thinking about. Take your lifetime of knowledge and infinite wisdom and make some solid goals for yourself. You have the luxury of having it all figured out. You know exactly what you love to do, what you don't and what you do very well. Do yourself and the world a favor and put it to good use. You have less time than you've ever had to do all these wonderful things so it dare not be wasted. Be mindful of every moment and take no day for granted. You should be spending your precious time doing things you love with true abandon.

We choose to look at it as full-time playfulness. This is what happens when you are able to set your own schedule. You PRIME it for the things you love as a priority and everything else takes a back seat. It's a time to refocus your energy on your passions first and life's work second.

REdirecting myself Towards Impassioned Recreational Exploits Daily

"Retirement, we understand, is great if you are busy, rich, and healthy. But then, under those conditions, work is great too."
Bill Vaughan

If the word RETIRED is not replaced by the time we enter that phase we will use it only as the acronym we've created above. When people ask us what we're doing we can tell them that we are indeed making the very best use of every minute and loving it. We are thrivers. This is how we've chosen to live our entire lives, so having a full and exciting retirement is a given. Our acronym pretty much says it all. It sounds exciting, shows passion for life and is clear that slowing down is not an option. We plan to live a retirement life that may exhaust – and hopefully inspire our grandchildren. Last but not least, its humorous and we take humor very seriously. Growing older is not for the fainthearted and humor becomes a necessity once you are redirecting yourself towards impassioned recreational exploits daily.

Back to the Future

Some people think that retirement means sitting around and doing nothing but watching TV all day. While they are fully engaged in couch potato mode they are probably eating more than necessary out of sheer boredom. As a result of this they will spend more time than they ever expected in the doctor's office. We don't know about you, but we're hoping to nurture some relationships when time affords us that option. Our doctors aren't one of those people on our list of top 10 people we want to be with. In fact, we're hoping he has to refer to our medical records to remember our names. Getting older has its fair share of unexpected physical challenges due to aging, but some are hastened by poor habits that directly affect our health. Even very young and fit athletes can suffer heart attacks and strokes due to hereditary conditions. We are not willing to gamble on our health or our genes. Not only do we want to be healthy for ourselves but we also want to be there for our spouse, kids and everyone that we cherish in our lives. Your excuse for not having time to exercise is gone now. Don't be selfish about your health. There are other people in your life that need you. Do it for them too. Not only will you be doing yourself and your body a favor, you'll also be setting a precedent for them to follow and be proud of.

Publicize Your Routine

As we've said before you should always make your routine public knowledge. Schedule time for your passions. It's your choice, but remember that you must have a plan. We would suggest beginning your retirement schedule in some aspects in the year prior to that final commute home. We all deal with major transitions better when they don't vary greatly from our current routine. Don't allow the temptation to waste your gift of extra time to creep into your thoughts. Plan for your own passions first so you can quickly realize the benefits of your new phase of life. Schedule time for your kids and/or grandkids, take long leisurely walks and enjoy nature, gardening or whatever else you desire.

Unprimed Seniors

"Father Time is not always a hard parent, and, though he tarries for none of his children, often lays his hand lightly upon those who have used him well; making them old men and women inexorably enough, but leaving their hearts and spirits young and in full vigour. With such people the grey head is but the impression of the old fellow's hand in giving them his blessing, and every wrinkle but a notch in the quiet calendar of a well-spent life."

If you don't PRIME your life this is what you'll be — one of the Unprimed Seniors. We all know at least one of them. They allow everyone else to dictate how their time is spent. The only time they will have to relax is on that rare occasion when no one else gives them something to do. Their kids label them as their permanent babysitter so they can enjoy their own time. The Unprimers will become resentful at some point. The boiling point usually erupts like clockwork in the middle of a big family holiday when stress is at its peak. Why are they always making the holiday meals at every turn? If there is no give and take then someone has allowed others to take more time from them than they should have. They must've failed to PRIME their life and make their priorities and plans public.

We prefer to be given Father Time's approval for having made the best use of our time.

Don't allow opportunistic people to manipulate your golden years. If you offer your time, that's one thing but having it snatched from right under your nose is another. If you are wasting your free time complaining to everyone about how much work, money and time you've committed to maintain the family holiday, then bring on the straightjacket, because you're headed for trouble. If you manage your time well, everyone will ultimately be happier because you will have satisfied all your needs first. You've heard this one before and it's so true; "If Mom isn't happy, no one's happy". This applies to those super grandpas also who organize huge family get-togethers to please everyone else and somehow don't get the help they bargained for from their kids.

Enjoy every minute of your retirement — you've earned it!

10. <u>EPILOG</u>

In Life And In Death

Karen writes: If we are afforded time before death or perhaps in an afterlife that lasts an eternity, how will we reflect on our time here on earth? For everyone the response will vary greatly depending on the quality and quantity of their life. We can't do so much about the quantity of our lives but we can do wonderful things about the quality of them. Accept discipline and your years will fly by as you cherish your past accomplishments and look forward with great excitement to your future ones.

Oh man, look out, here comes that metaphorical truck that is responsible for so many hypothetical deaths! Splat. Yeah, that **was** me probably running out to the curb to get the latest manuscript & trying to keep my dog from bolting into the street after me and getting run over by the FedEx truck. My first thought would be "God, maybe you misunderstood when I asked you to help me write a killer book. And those comments about this book being the death of me were just jokes! I did always want to be thinner, so I got that going for me now, um, thanks." The laughter stops and my life flashes before me and I'm left to deal with the reality of seeing what is now my past life. I have died happy. I can honestly say I have lived a very full, exciting and happy life and that is an accomplishment I can be proud of - forever. My time on earth was well-spent.

Regrets are about something that we didn't do. My biggest regret will not be for what I haven't done, but for what I will not be able to do now that I'm gone. If you have regrets in life it's not too late to do something about them.

To be able to teach anything you have to bring real life experience to the class. I have learned that it took a string of accomplishments on an ongoing basis to keep me fulfilled and happy. Harris is right. It **is** all about accomplishments and to achieve them throughout your entire life. Discipline applied liberally will guarantee your life is happy before and after the "truck of death" comes down your street.

We hope that others will continue to learn as we have about the virtues of being disciplined. We just prefer they learn it when they are very young so they can experience their own best life by living it well - always.

The Legacy

"You begin saving the world by saving one person at a time; all else is grandiose romanticism or politics."
Charles Bukowski

Harris writes: What else could I possibly want out of life? Why can't I just kick back and take it easy? I've done it all. I've accomplished every goal both personal and professional. So, enough is enough, right? What could possibly top the success I have already achieved? The answer is quite simple. I've been saying it to my friends for decades but didn't realize the impact of it until now, at the ripe old age of 48.

If I cross the street tomorrow and get run over by my "truck of death" it's not enough that the people I've mentored in discipline will have something for the rest of their lives to remember me by. It's not enough that I've made them productive or that I've helped them to help themselves become successful, etc. I want more! I want to have a major impact on people that I've never met before. I want to be remembered by one word and that's discipline. Many people need guidance to make the most out of their existence. I want them to turn to discipline now and even when I'm long gone.

Right now the word discipline is rarely used at home or at the office. The most common place you hear it is when professional athletes are in rigorous training or occasionally at the gym amongst some hard-core bodybuilders. Mentioned elsewhere it is usually in the context of "old school" discipline. That's because it used to be a requirement for everyday survival in the "old days", but society has changed so rapidly that we have lost sight of this gem. We feel that discipline should be taught at home to every child. Actually "teaching" kids is probably the wrong word, you would teach your kids about the facts of life or about manners at the dinner table, etc. As discussed earlier in the book, mentoring children on the importance of discipline at a young age is the best gift a parent can give to their son or daughter.

147

My ultimate goal is to leave a legacy behind. It is no longer about just completing goals. Bernard Shaw says it best below."

"This is the true joy in life, the being recognized by yourself as a mighty one; the being thoroughly worn out before you are thrown on the scrap heap; the being a force of nature instead of a feverish selfish little clod of ailments and grievances complaining that the world will not devote itself to making you happy.

I am of the opinion that my life belongs to the whole community and as long as I live it is my privilege to do for whatever I can. I want to be thoroughly used up when I die for the harder I work the more I live. I rejoice in life for it's own sake. Life is no brief candle to me. It is a sort of splendid torch which I have got hold of for the moment, and I want to make it burn as brightly as possible before handing it on to future generations."
Bernard Shaw

Do It For The Children

Parents want the very best for their kids. There is no greater gift that you can pass on to your kids than discipline. It's a multifaceted and beautiful thing. First of all, it's an immediate reward in itself to see their face light up when they apply it for themselves and realize the impact it can have. Secondly, your life will be infinitely easier if you've disciplined your child from the start because everyone will be happier and well-adjusted. Third, you need to do it for society. What do you want to contribute to society? A happy, well-adjusted child that contributes to society or one that struggles at every turn. If you are not disciplined yourself then don't expect your kids to be. It doesn't mean that every disciplined parent will end up with a disciplined child. Each individual is built differently. If you want to give them every advantage in life teaching them discipline is the way to go. They have to be taught this ongoing lesson at every opportunity, but they have to be ready to learn it. Don't make the assumption that they will learn this stuff from others, because it's your responsibility and the odds of that happening are pretty slim. It should come from you, but if another close family member or friend is willing, allow them to instill these ideas into their minds also over time. More role models are always better. They are watching and learning from you every minute.

Spend Time On Your Kids, Not Money

> "If you want your children to turn out well, spend twice as much time with them and half as much money."
> *Anonymous*

Time is what your kids need and want from you. This is one of the biggest reasons why you must PRIME your life so you have ample time to spend with your kids. They don't want or need your money. In a San Diego Union-Tribune article titled, "Don't Give Your Kids Too Much, Experts Say" this topic was covered beautifully, here it is in its entirety:

Not long ago parents believed they could help their children succeed in the world by giving them every opportunity, from summer camp to college. But now as we straddle the 20th and 21st centuries, a period of unprecedented affluence and consumerism, parents are starting to wonder. Are we actually depriving our kids by giving them too much? Too much stuff, too many after-school activities and too much financial support?

We worry that excess will kill off motivation and initiative, those things that make up our financial values. Giving kids too much, says Encinitas psychiatrist Dr. Robert J. Solomon, can interfere with their development because it creates complacency. "It's a mistake," he says. "They need to be a little hungry."

This overindulgence can affect almost any income bracket. Janet Bodnar, senior editor and resident kids expert at *Kiplinger's Personal Finance* magazine, writes that "no matter what your income, any amount of money can be toxic, if you lavish too much of it on your kids."

149

Alice B. Reinig, a San Diego psychologist who consults with families and family businesses, says that almost anyone can spoil a child. All you have to do is "give them what they want, without them having to put out a lot to get it."

Always giving in to a child's requests is often a parent's easiest way out. But, she says, "It's a quick fix, as opposed to dealing with the emotions behind the request. They will not have a resource in their pocket when times are hard."

By fulfilling every whim, we deprive children of several things: an appreciation for individual items and experiences; the motivation to accomplish; the value of frustration; the pride in perseverance despite obstacles, and the joy of achieving a hard-won goal.

"If they have not learned to earn things, they can feel entitled" to them, Reinig says. "They don't appreciate people and things."

So how can we banish complacency? Return the PlayStation 2 and cancel the ski trip? Not necessarily. It's not about how many things you give your children or do for them. It's your attitude. "It's not the money," says Valerie Jacobs, a San Diego psychologist and wealth counselor. "It's how you raise them."

Here are some pointers:

- **Communicate with your kids early and often**. Talk about money, about how you earn it and how you plan to spend it. Parents shouldn't be afraid to comment on the good and bad financial practices of other families, as well as on ethical issues. And when your children ask questions, answer them in an age-appropriate fashion. Avoiding the subject of money can make it seem dirty or shameful.
- **Be a good role model**. Children simply won't buy the philosophy of "do as I say, not as I do."
- **Actively encourage good values**. Jacobs, whose personal stake in her Los Angeles engineering company founded by her father is worth millions, consciously works at inculcating her family's work ethic into her two children. She and her husband made clear to their son he wouldn't be getting a new car when he turned 16, but rather permission to drive the family's 8-year-old minivan. He got his first jobs with no family help, scooping ice cream and parking cars.
- **Set limits**. When our parents used to say they couldn't afford something, it was often true. But today many parents can't

employ that old standby when their children ask them to buy something. Parents need to develop their own terminology for these occasions. You could say, "No, that's a want, not a need." And stick to your guns. You might also say that the item isn't in your budget – and let them learn what a budget is by receiving a weekly allowance.

- **Have them manage money now**. Most parents would never let a teenager get behind the wheel of a car without taking lessons, getting some practice and earning a driver's license. Yet these same parents might send their kids off to college or live on their own without the necessary money skills. Every kid should have an allowance, whether or not it's tied to doing chores, to learn money management.

- **Give children responsibility**. This allows them to develop a sense of competency and self-sufficiency, important skills for school and work. Have them set the table, take out the trash or help with a pet.

- **Don't choose your child's career**. Especially if you're successful, your child might want to excel in a different field. "The most important thing parents can do for their children is to help them find their passion in life," says Solomon. When parents exert too much pressure, he says, "You end up with a lot of very unhappy kids and adults."

- **Teach them about charity**. Peg and Bob Eddy, certified financial planners who run Creative Capital Management in San Diego, started when their two sons, now grown, were in grade school. The boys chose a charity and the Eddys would send a check in their names. They "adopted" families through church during the holidays; one year they cleaned up the Civic Concourse after homeless people camped there on Christmas. As they grew older, the boys took charge themselves, sponsoring clothes and food drives in high school. Now in their 20s, both continue to do volunteer work. The Eddys are setting up a $1,000 annual scholarship in the name of each son at their high school – with the hope that their sons will one day contribute as well.

Take it upon yourself to make it a goal NOT to spoil your kids by lavishing too much money on them. Some parents use it as an excuse because they claim they have more money than time. This is because they've made their careers a priority instead of their kids. PRIME your life accordingly and make the time. They are onto you like white on rice and are much more perceptive than we give them credit for. They will take full advantage of you when you are most vulnerable. Most of the time it's not the toy that they want, its time spent with you driving to the store that they wouldn't get otherwise. Don't underestimate their intelligence at any age. They are getting a two-for-one deal at your expense and you are putty in their cute little hands. Sheer manipulation in pursuit of every kids dream – more time AND more stuff to play with.

It doesn't mean you can't give your kids nice things; just don't give them more than they need. The amount of money you make should not be an issue, unless you allow it to be. My daughter is 5 and already knows that she will not be driving a new car until she can afford to pay for one herself like we both did. She began making comments about the cars she wanted when she reaches 16 because we play "name that car" since we are classic car enthusiasts. We felt a dose of reality and hunger-building conversation couldn't hurt. Now her comments turn to how hard the driver of that car must've worked and wondering what they do for a living. We just hope that whatever they do is something they love and that they are happy, because it's never about "the car". We focus on the exciting journey of getting the car of your dreams. We talk about appreciation for everything we have on a regular basis because we want her to know that we worked a long time before we earned the things we have.

> "A master can tell you what he expects of you. A teacher, though, awakens your own expectations."
> *Patricia Neal*

Please mentor children. The more kids we mentor on the importance of acquiring discipline the brighter their future will look. Harris writes: As discussed in my first book someone mentored me when I was 13 and it changed my life forever. <u>Thirteen is the prime of your life for learning and realizing the benefits of discipline.</u> Thirteen is the age where it all begins. It sets precedence for the rest of your life. Without someone taking the time to mentor me, it would have been extremely difficult to get to the level I am today. I would have wasted much of my lifetime probably getting into trouble with the law, or doing drugs, etc., like many of my friends in Junior High School. Discipline should be taught at an early age if at all possible, but don't shove it down someone's throat – you need to start out slowly and gradually take on more.

> "There comes that Mysterious Meeting in your Life when Someone Acknowledges who we are and

what we can be By Igniting the Circuits of Our Highest Potential."
Mahatma Gandhi

My mentor started out slowly by teaching me what discipline was all about and what it could do for my life. At first he may have taken it easy on me but he didn't baby me – he made it clear that certain things wouldn't be tolerated like if I was late to one of our appointments. In the beginning of our mental and physical training sessions (training the mind and body) he made it very clear to me that if I was late just one time our training sessions were over. There would be no second chances. He didn't say it a nice way but a very direct and stern way. His mannerisms were that of a drill sergeant and his physique was statuesque like that of a Greek God. So how could I not listen?

"The greatest good you can do for another is not just share your riches, but reveal to them their own."
Benjamin Disraeli

One of the greatest gifts anyone can give back to society is mentoring children about the benefits of discipline. If children are mentored when they're young like I was, their life will be rewarding. If you can give your son, daughter, or neighbor only one gift let it be the knowledge of discipline.

"Children have never been very good at listening to their elders, but they have never failed to imitate them."
James Arthur Baldwin

Eldership

What are some of the things you think of when you hear the word elder? How about:

> *Wise*
> *Respected*
> *Mature*

> *Dignitary*
> *Statesman*
> *Class act*
> *Distinguished*

We can go on and on. Eldership has nothing to do with age. It's symbolic of someone who has been there and done that. Beyond that they are ready and willing to teach you every gritty detail that is required to elevate you into being an elder yourself one day. Their hand is readily extended to you if they feel you have potential and you are up for the challenge. It's important to note their position on the ladder in relation to where you are standing. If they are at the top of the proverbial ladder and you are closer to the bottom, then they will give you a map or show you the way. If you are not far from where they are, then they will guide you up or give you direction as to where you should step next. In any case, you will have to take those steps yourself because elders prefer to watch you learn for yourself. They are masters at helping others come to their own conclusions. That's what makes their lessons so valuable. It provides hands-on experience for the student and the joy of sharing knowledge for the elder.

If you pass on this once in a lifetime offer you can kiss that golden opportunity goodbye. What are the odds of lightning striking in the same place twice? The Elder won't have to look far to find someone else who can benefit from his or her knowledge. All of us can benefit from having more discipline in our lives. Those who possess it will be led onto less traveled roads by virtue of the fact that true discipline is unconventional. It's also timeless and therefore it's always in demand. Those few who are in demand can afford the luxury of options and the freedom of choice for two reasons. First, they are always looking for opportunities to apply themselves and satisfy their thirst for knowledge. Second, they are being sought out by those elders who choose to surround themselves with others who aren't afraid of jumping into uncharted waters for the opportunity to give it all they've got and learn something new. It's not just about thinking outside of the box, it's more about living on the edge of the box because that provides a perfect vantage point for the constant flow of ideas and opportunities from both sides. Being open to opportunities is what it's all about.

There is no better mentor than one who teaches you through example in such a methodical yet nonchalant fashion that it all appears as easy as breathing. You know better though, because in all your life you have come across very few whom you can call true elders in every sense of the word. These are the special ones, the teachers who sneak wisdom between your ears when you aren't looking. They are willing to give their precious gift of time towards making someone else's life better because someone in their life had taken the time to do the same for them. They will never forget their mentor or the impact they had on their lives. So this is now their goal to "pay it forward" as often as is humanly possible because this is what life is all about. Achieving your own goals in your youth and continually helping others achieve theirs through sharing your collective wisdom time and again.

An article in the San Diego Union Tribune told of a couple of elders who are staying young via their eldership work. Together, Vic Arballo and Woody Grindle account for 155 years. Vic's 72; Woody – 83. But neither one looks his age.

"If you want to stay young, get involved in the Laubach Literacy Council program," says Vic. This is delivered so sincerely from the distinguished looking retired businessman that, at first, you miss seeing the impression his tongue leaves in his cheek:

Its always a sure bet, you tell yourself, that spry, healthy-looking guys into their seventh and eighth decades would have some plausible slant on how to age gracefully. But what could they have found in a 16-year-old project that, on its surface, teaches mainly foreign-born adults how to read English, not how to find the fountain of youth?

"It's the exhilaration of working closely with someone who needs your help, and giving them exactly what they need," says Woody. "That always keeps you young – I feel like I'm 25." "So do I," adds Vic. Indeed, over the life of the program at the Chula Vista Literacy Center, located at the Community Congregational Church of Chula Vista, the two pals have taught more than 800 adults how to read – and read well.

They've also trained more than 300 tutors. They hooked up as the program's co-directors soon after Woody started the center as an outreach of the church in 1986. Vic, semi retired then, answered one of Woody's ads seeking tutors. He never forgets what spurred him to respond.

His dad, J.C. Arballo, an intensely compassionate man, instilled him with a desire to look out for others. And as a Boy Scout of 14, he helped organize and establish a new troop in a disadvantaged section of his hometown Chula Vista that was widely known as a pit of crime and other anti-social behavior. The troop didn't last more than a few years. But during its run, it clearly helped steer a number of young boys away from street life. And every time he considered that – even as a teen – Vic would feel an uplifting rush inside.

On the day that he read Woody's ad, he says, he felt that jolt again and it told him that "this was another similar opportunity to help people and I had to take it." Vic had never formally taught reading or any other subject before. But Woody, who'd trained as a tutor through the Laubach Literacy Council program, taught him well.

Students kept coming into the center, and soon Vic was teaching classes of nearly 40 mostly non-English speakers. Their reading levels varied from beginners to intermediate and advanced. "I had to design lessons that could reach all levels, and I was teaching them how to read, write and speak English," he says. "It was a tremendous challenge...But I could see how I was helping people. And even now I still enjoy teaching."

Now consider Woody. He and Dotty, his wife, have been married for 62 years. Long ago, in working to keep their union strong, Woody learned how to recognize when his wife needed a boost. In those times, he would dig down and find what was needed in him. He found, too, that when Dotty was OK, he was OK.

Six years ago, Dotty, now 79, suffered a stroke on Woody's birthday and he went right to work, soon afterward, helping her to regain speech and motor skills. The retired aeronautical engineer even improvised and designed equipment that aided in his wife's rehabilitation, and today, the two are back doing their favorite things again – together. When you're happy, Woody, Dotty and Vic will tell you, it keeps you feeling young; and doing good for others keeps you happy.

Consider yourself blessed for having elders in your life. These are people who give us endless reasons to look forward to our elder years so we can be like them. If nothing else, just for the thrill of being looked at with that same admiration that we felt while being mentored by them. If you are disciplined you will believe in yourself. Having someone else believe in you is virtually unforgettable.

This is why you must strive to be an elder. It is the very best of all possible worlds. It's the icing on the cake of life. Giving is always better than receiving, but when you know that the receiver will continue to give your knowledge long after you're gone; then it's simply priceless. Worth every minute, or dollar, depending on how much a minute is worth to you.

HK'S ANECDOTES

HK'S MOST COMMON PHRASES OF THE UNPRIMED:

> ## I Take Life One Day At A Time

If you sincerely want to get ahead and make something of your life you need a well thought-out plan. Nobody has ever become successful by doing the above. Success is measured by lifelong accomplishments and acquiring a certain level of discipline. This cannot be achieved by taking one day at a time. Every minute of the day and every day of the year needs to be planned and accounted for. This phrase is meant for someone recovering from a major illness or getting over a traumatic experience.

> ## It Can Wait Till Tomorrow

I hate when people tell me tomorrow is another day - relax! With that kind of attitude you might as well wait till next week. What's the difference? For me every minute of every day is precious and once wasted will <u>never</u> come back. Don't keep pushing things off till the next day – you will never get ahead. As a matter of fact, you will only get further and further behind. You should have a sense of urgency for everyday of the year. With a laid back attitude accomplishments will be few and far between.

> ## I Need At Least Eight Hours Of Sleep Each Night

You complain there's never enough time in a day to get everything you need done but on the other hand you sleep 8-9 hours every night and probably more on the weekend. As highlighted throughout the book you need to do more with less resource. Who has the luxury of sleeping 8 hours a day anymore? Even if you do have the time, I think your time could be better spent. So-called sleep experts say you need at least 8 hours. I disagree. I've been living on 4 hours sleep for the past 15 years. There's no reason why you can't cut your sleep back by 1 hour a night and see if that works for you. Just think about all the goals you could be working on with that extra 7 hours a week.

➢ I Can't Do It

No real explanation required. If you haven't got what it takes, then step aside and take a back seat. Cruel words? Not really, if you want to keep on doing the same routine day in and day out, always keeping things simple, and afraid to take on new challenges. For many of you that want to excel and start making the most out of your life all of your dreams can become a reality with discipline.

➢ What Are Your New Year's Resolutions

Why do people waste their time making up New Year's resolutions year after year? Have you ever tried to complete a major goal at work without a formal project plan? Then how can you make up a goal at the spur of the moment and expect to actually accomplish it without a well thought out plan? And, if you need to start a goal based on a special day then chances are you will not be successful in your endeavor. Goals should be established if and only if they're part of your PRIME.

➢ I'm Too Tired To Exercise

Who isn't too tired to exercise? There are dozens of excuses that anyone can think of on any given day for not exercising. The number one reason to do it consistently is to keep you healthy. I typically exercise from 4-6am every morning, it's a great way to start the day and it sets the tempo. By 6am the wheels are spinning at full speed. I don't need a cup of coffee to wake me up. There are better and healthier ways to get yourself going each morning. Make it a point to find what works for you. You will not believe the benefits until you apply them for yourself.

➢ I Don't Feel Good

I can think of at least a hundred times in a year that I don't feel very well (upset stomach, headache, general aches and pains, etc.) but it doesn't mean that everyone has to know about it or that I'm going to sit there and feel sorry for myself. Just the opposite should happen.

Tell yourself to get off your lazy butt and make something happen. Don't dwell on pain, work right through it.

In general people whine too much. Society has turned most of us into wimps. You always hear people complaining about all their aches and pains. They want you to feel sorry for them. I guess that old saying "misery loves company" holds true. I'm 48 years old and have all kinds of aches and pains but that's for me and only for me. I just keep telling myself that I cannot be broken over and over again and then go attack the day.

➤ It's Not Whether You Win Or Lose, It's How You Play The Game

It's always about winning and it should always be about winning! No one should ever feel good about losing! Yes, we should play by the rules and apply our values at all times while doing our very best to win. All I'm saying is that you should always play to win. Winning can be just as habit forming as losing. They are both very addictive so take your pick. It is better to train your mind in a positive way by telling yourself that you will win and take every step to reach that goal. If you simply follow the words of the above phrase throughout life then you may never really give it everything you've got to reach your goals, minor and major. If you have honestly given your best and lost at something, then you can say you really did play to win and next time you will try harder and yes, you played the game as best as you could.

➤ I'm So Stressed Out - I Need A Vacation

The word "stress" has been over utilized for the past few decades now. We all have problems (personal, health, financial, etc.) and there are some days when those problems are unbearable. When you acquire discipline and are able to train your mind to effectively and efficiently manage your life the 'S' word will no longer be in your vocabulary. The majority of people are stressed because they have failed to manage their time well. Goal-setting and priorities aligned correctly will significantly decrease your self-induced stress.

➤ Be Happy With What You Have

You should <u>never</u> be happy with what you have. I'm not talking about material things. I'm talking about accomplishments, your position in a corporation, your life, etc. Always strive for more – once your mind has been trained (see Chapter 6) it will always be hungry for more. You will have no choice - so don't bother fighting it. I get a major rush every time I accomplish something so why would I ever want that feeling to stop. You can have anything you want, whether they be material things or not. If you work hard enough you will be much happier with even the tiniest goals because of the string of accomplishments that were fulfilled to reach them.

➢ Stop And Smell The Roses

In this day and age when you're asked to do more with less time there is less time to "stop and smell the roses". This quote has been around for ages. It originated back when people had the luxury to appreciate the beauty and simple joys life much more often. Because we work so hard it appears that we don't take time to do this, but that couldn't be further from the truth. Our motivation for working hard is so we can spend ample time playing. If you follow your PRIME and prioritize your life you will be managing your life much more efficiently and if you decide to build it into your schedule there's no reason why you can't stop and smell the roses more often. We prefer not to stop for too long, because we like to smell as many roses as we can! That means we might be biking, hiking, 4-wheeling, planting or jogging by those roses, but we're all over this one. We make it a goal to enjoy life's pleasures everyday. We are big sunrise and sunset fans, walk our kids to school to enjoy nature while we exercise and spend quality time. We play hard on our weekends. Make the time.

➢ Failure Is Ok But Giving Up Is Unacceptable

Don't ever tell yourself that failure is ok. It's not ok! If you fail once you run the risk of repeating it. Be afraid to death of failure. It is the worst thing that could possibly happen. Scare yourself into thinking that if you fail once you may set yourself up for an endless string of upsets in the future. Do or say whatever you want to make sure you don't fail. DO whatever it takes to ensure success!

➢ Dieting

Don't! Just start eating right. Diets don't work for a prolonged period of time. They're only temporary solutions to a lifelong problem. The solution is making health (consistently exercising and eating right) a priority in your life.

➢ <u>I Need A Day Off</u>

Why? Are you feeling stressed? Are you feeling rundown? Get with it and stop fantasizing. This is the 21st century where you <u>need to</u> do more with less. Can you afford to take a day off every time you feel tired? You will <u>need to</u> continuously push yourself even on those days you're feeling run down. Most people will tell you the opposite and take an R&R day. Build that R&R day into your PRIME at regularly scheduled intervals.

➢ <u>Retirement</u>

Why? To play golf everyday, go fishing everyday, or get up and do nothing. Wow how exciting! I don't like the word retirement because it carries such a negative message. I know it may sound harsh, but in my opinion retirement or letting your mind go dormant is such a waste. I can see taking it easy a bit when you start getting up there in age but don't stop production altogether. Hey, you can still play golf a few days a week, but don't sit around and turn that wonderful mind of yours completely off. There's still so much for you to accomplish.

➢ <u>My Intentions Were There</u>

> "Begin somewhere.
> You cannot build a reputation on what you intend to do."
> *Liz Smith*

Intentions don't mean anything. Anyone can have as many intentions as they can dream up, but where the rubber meets the road is when you follow through with each and every commitment. Failure to follow through on just one commitment is <u>wrong</u> and you will quickly lose respect from your friends and colleagues. You will be labeled as just a talker. It's sad to say but I've come across quite a few people that fit that category.

➢ <u>Pinning False Hopes on the New Year</u>

Good wishes around the holidays won't change a thing. Some of my favorites are: "I hope you have a good New Year and I hope this New Year brings you good health, happiness, and success." Folks you need to get a grip here. Mere words alone will not give you a better life. It's not the well-wishers I'm aggravated with it's those who really think the calendar is going to change their lives! And hoping and praying won't do it either. Do you think because it's January 1st that you will have a chance for a fresh start in life? Please tell me what the difference between December 31st and January 1st is. It's a day – that's it. As I mention throughout the book it takes hard work to change your life around, not some silly date on the calendar.

➤ <u>**Big Is Beautiful**</u>

If you're overweight don't con yourself into believing that being fat is beautiful. Let's stop playing make believe because being overweight is not beautiful and more importantly it's extremely unhealthy. If you keep telling yourself that it's beautiful you'll never lose the weight. Look in the mirror and be honest with yourself. Be dissatisfied. If you are unhappy with how you look and your health is being compromised then it's time to start doing something about it. Do yourself a favor and seek help through a counselor, support group or exercise program. You owe it to yourself to treat your body with respect and take care of it. People care about you and your health.

➤ <u>**I Hope...**</u>

This is only reserved for those times when things are totally out of your control, i.e., someone is ill or is suffering through a trauma, etc. Don't spend your entire life hoping things are going to happen to you. Work your PRIME so things do happen for you. You are in control of your life, no one else. Just being hopeful instead of supporting your goals with a plan guarantees that you will feel hopeless for a good portion of your existence.

HK'S FAVORITE REMARKS:

➤ <u>**Whatever It Takes**</u>

> "Hell, there are no rules here – we're trying to accomplish something."
> *Thomas A. Edison*

Simply put, you need to do whatever it takes to complete a goal or project on schedule. Just completing a goal is not enough, do whatever it takes to complete a goal by its scheduled due date. When trying to accomplish your goals Thomas Edison said it best above "There are no rules here". Do whatever it takes to complete a goal. I probably use this quote more than any other quote because I truly believe that's what made me successful. I was <u>always</u> doing whatever it takes.

➢ <u>Just Do It</u>

> "Action is eloquence."
> *William Shakespeare*

If you think you can do it then make it happen BUT you must be committed and be sure it fits into your PRIME. Don't take on challenges for the sake of putting another notch on the belt. Besides PRIME there has to be commitment and passion behind each and every goal.

➢ <u>Nothing Worthwhile Comes Easy-You Need To Earn It.</u>

Acquiring discipline is hard work and not much fun in the beginning, it will force you to put structure into your life. It means being on a strict routine everyday of the week, and yes that includes weekends. You're now on the clock, where every minute has a price tag. You're suddenly managing your life as if it were a business. Sure it's hard work, but nothing in your lifetime will be this rewarding. It will change your life forever and for the better! One of the biggest mistakes society makes is not teaching the benefits of discipline in school. The best-case scenario would be if parents taught this to their children and mentored them along with age appropriate classes.

➢ <u>No Pain, No Gain</u>

To be successful in life means acquiring discipline. It will <u>not</u> be easy especially in the first year or so. Acquiring discipline is <u>hard</u> work. This is reality and I don't want to sugarcoat the effort. But to us (and we hope for most of you reading this) what's a little pain and hard work for something this worthwhile?

➢ <u>Winning Is Everything</u>

Winning is everything and the sooner you get used to winning on a regular basis the more success you will enjoy. The more wins you get, the more you want, it becomes addictive. This goes for your personal life as well as your professional life.

➢ <u>Training The Mind</u>

To be successful in life the mind has to be the pilot. It has all the power and controls. It will take you anywhere and everywhere, and if trained properly it will put your body in autopilot to help you take on your daily battles. It will never get tired or falter. Training the mind is the most critical aspect of acquiring discipline, which is why it's the theme of this book.

➢ <u>Time Is Money</u>

You need to equate every minute to a dollar figure. The same way you would budget your finances to make every dollar count; every minute of your life needs to be managed properly and efficiently. Time is the most valuable resource you have!

➢ <u>Success Is Not About Money</u>

Success is all about accomplishments and being able to take your mind and body to new heights. With accomplishments there are rewards. There is no greater feeling in the world then completing another one of your goals ahead of schedule. On many instances a by-product of some of these accomplishments is monetary but that comes with the territory. Success is having discipline. Discipline is being able to accomplish whatever you want, whenever you want. Accomplishments last an eternity but money comes and goes.

HK'S TIME WASTELAND:

➤ <u>Kids Playing Unlimited Video Games</u>

Ever since video games hit the scene teenagers spend more time playing games than trying to figure out what they want to do when they grow up. They usually wait until they've graduated from high school. This is too late! Teenagers need to start thinking about their future career when they're sophomores and juniors in high school. Parents – please start mentoring these kids.

➤ <u>Watching A 3-4 Hour Sporting Event On TV</u>

How many people sit in front of the TV every weekend and watch sporting events for hours on end? Then they complain there are never enough hours in a day. If you're a sports fan that's fine, but don't allow it to suck endless hours of your life away. Should this be a priority for you? Are you getting what you want out of it? Is there a sport that you can play instead of the many that you are sitting on the couch watching? If you're a family man, it's worth thinking about seriously. You're sending a clear message to your kids that it's perfectly fine to vegetate for hours on end instead of being active with your family. Your choice. Remember it's your life, and theirs.

➤ <u>Sitting In Commute Traffic Everyday</u>

What a waste of time! Why can't you get up earlier and beat the traffic? If you don't have to drop your kids off at school at a certain hour, or drop your significant other off at work and have no other responsibilities in the morning then it's silly to sit in commute traffic. Get up an hour earlier and cut a significant amount of time off your commute. Use it to catch up on some work in the office.

➤ <u>Sitting At The Airport For Hours Or On A Long Flight Doing Absolutely Nothing</u>

Since September 11th, 2001 airports have got to be one of the most miserable places to be in. You need to get there several hours before your flight just to check-in. Then you usually have to wait in a very long, painful, and agonizing security line. On top of all that there are usually delays. Don't go to the airport empty-handed; bring some of your work along. Times have changed so you need to be prepared. Don't just sit there for hours looking at other people and the artwork on the walls.

➤ <u>Going To The Health Club For The First 2 Weeks In January</u>

Have you ever noticed how busy it is at health clubs around the first of the year? I have no idea why these people even bother going except to try and fulfill their New Year's resolutions. As I discussed earlier in the book New Year's resolutions have no substance. These establishments feed off of this whole idea of getting in shape for the New Year. Don't fall victim to this advertising bonanza that capitalizes on those who actually believe that this magical date will suddenly free them from the obstacles that have kept them away from the gym every other day of the year.

➤ <u>Taking Your Car To The Car Wash</u>

Why can't you do it yourself? I live in Los Angeles and rarely do you see people washing their own cars. You can add another reason to that long list of why so many Americans are out of shape. Why not look at it as exercise? God knows we all need it. In the brutal winter months where weather is more of an issue it's understandable, but certainly NOT in warm weather states.

➤ <u>Standing In Long Lines</u>

I always have more important things to do besides standing around in long lines. Whether it's for grocery shopping, going out to dinner, movie, nightclub, etc. I won't do it-anything over 15 minutes, forget it. I won't go to restaurants and grocery shopping during peak hours. For newly released movies-forget it – I prefer to wait a few weeks until the crowds are gone. If you MUST stand in line i.e., groceries then you can speed up the process for everyone by always helping those before you in line to put their groceries on the conveyer belt. I'm just standing there, so why not help someone else? It makes me feel good and I get to the checkout that much quicker. My son witnesses the instant gratification of helping others as a bonus.

➢ <u>Waiting For People Who Are Late For An Appointment</u>

> "Punctuality is one of the cardinal business virtues:
> always insist on it in your subordinates."
> *Don Marquis*

The easiest commitment to keep is being punctual, yet so many people take this part of this discipline so lightly. They have so many excuses; traffic, couldn't get off the phone with a customer, etc. and in their eyes all excuses are legitimate. I beg to differ; <u>no</u> excuses are reasonable unless of course, it's some kind of personal emergency. It truly drives me crazy when people are late for appointments. It's totally unacceptable.

HK'S QUOTES:

➢ <u>I Cannot Be Broken</u>

On those days when I hurt, am tired, or a combination of both my body and mind are at odds. My body is telling me to rest and my mind is telling me to keep going. My mind <u>always</u> wins. We've all been there on those days when we needed that little extra push. I tell myself over and over again that I cannot be broken. It motivates me to forget about any potential pains I may have on any given day.

➢ <u>I'll Sleep Plenty When I Die</u>

When my friends or family tell me to rest, they know the line that's coming right back at them, think about it for a minute – it's true isn't it? It's one of my favorite and most frequently used phrases.

➢ <u>It's Me Against Me</u>

I am my biggest enemy. Everyday when I wake up I go into battle with myself. I beat myself up mentally to adhere to my priorities and to conquer my goals at an accelerated rate. There's a sense of urgency everyday of my life. Life is a one-time event and I make every minute count.

➤ <u>Accomplishments Are Fulfilling, Relaxation Is A Temporary Feeling</u>

Life is all about accomplishments. There is no greater feeling in the world than accomplishing your greatest aspirations. Without accomplishments life is just existing. With accomplishments you grow and life is worthwhile.

➤ <u>Status Quo Is No Different Than Death</u>

Doing the same routine day in and day out, year after year - how boring that must be. Get real, get with it – time is so precious, make something happen.

➤ <u>Content Free Speech</u>

These are those people that are good talkers but have no substance behind their words. You know those individuals that promise the world but never deliver. Talk is cheap.

➤ <u>Do I Want To Look Like Millions Of Other Out Of Shape Americans</u>

Eighty percent of exercising is mental. When I train people in the gym part of the training is mental as well as physical. I play all these little mind games with them. I ask them "how badly do they want to change the way you look or do you want to look like most other Americans?" Look at your out of shape co-workers, friends, and family – do you want to look like them? I'm not saying this in a disrespectful way. –I'm just playing mind games to try and help them to motivate themselves.

➤ <u>Don't Dwell On It</u>

When personal issues arise regardless of the severity don't dwell on it. You're wasting precious time. Get over it quickly and get on with your life. If you can't walk away or let go of the issue and you feel that strongly about it don't sit there whining and complaining. You have a purpose and if you're trying to acquire discipline you are on a mission. Stay focused and don't let anyone or anything get in your way.

➢ <u>Never Give Up</u>

> "It's always too early to quit."
> *Norman Vincent Peale*

Whatever challenges you take on, regardless of the obstacles that lie before you, or the degree of difficulty, if you want it and it's part of your PRIME then be persistent – don't quit.

> Most of the important things in the world have been accomplished by people who have kept on trying when there seemed to be no hope at all.
> *Dale Carnegie*

➢ <u>Treat All Days Equally</u>

In this era everyone has been asked to do more with less as we mentioned in the beginning of the book. Very few people can actually take the entire weekend off and do whatever they wanted or perhaps do nothing every Saturday and Sunday. If you want to accomplish more and fulfill all of your dreams you need to start looking at a 6 day work week and look forward to 1 day off for personal time, friends, or quality time with the family.

➢ <u>If I Didn't Exercise Every Time I Was In Pain, Sick, Or Feeling Tired I Would Never Exercise</u>

When you hit your mid to late 30's, 40's and beyond occasional aches and pains become a part of life. We're speaking from experience. Exercise through these minor discomforts, otherwise they will become just another excuse for abandoning exercise altogether. You know how we feel about that idea! It's no exercise at all that causes more than it's fair share of aches, pains and health issues.

HK'S GRIEVANCES

➢ Cell Phones In The Gym

When it's time to exercise make every moment count especially if health and fitness are one of your priorities. Although I have a cell phone and use it profusely I realize they're annoying to those around me. When most people go to the gym they're focusing on their routine. It's very distracting to hear phones ringing. It's even worse having to listen to someone gabbing away while you are trying to focus and concentrate. Please keep them out of the gym as a courtesy to others.

➢ Using Automated Walkways In Airports And Luggage With Wheels

Everyone complains that it's almost impossible to exercise when they travel. I travel every week and I still hand carry my garment bag and computer bag while walking at a brisk pace without the aid of automated walkways. Most people today are pulling their bags on wheels and walking on automated walkways. Only utilize them when it's impossible to carry everything yourself.

➢ Personal Trainers

Personal trainers are great for beginners. This is especially true when one doesn't know the routine. But the biggest problem people make is mixing up learning the routine with becoming dependent on a trainer just because they don't have the drive to make it on their own. Their logic is; if they don't have the discipline and they can never get disciplined then why bother? They can just pay someone to push them.

Start training the mind – it's equally as important. Do not hire a trainer for more than 6 weeks. Once that person understands the routine, then they should cut the cord and start motivating themselves.

➤ <u>Never Use An Escalator If Stairs Are Available</u>

There's <u>always</u> time to get some type of exercise even if you have a busy schedule. Many of the buildings I visit have only 2, 3, or 4 flights of stairs – so take those stairs – every little bit counts. Don't be lazy. The same goes for department stores or subway stations. Take the stairs whenever possible. Your body will thank you.

➤ <u>Feeling Sorry For Yourself</u>

Whether you're having a bad day at work or you're a bit under the weather, feeling sorry for yourself or having other people pity you will only make matters worse. It just makes you weaker mentally. The more mentally tough you are the faster you'll recover. Get off your lazy butt and make something positive happen!

➤ <u>Brown-Nosing The Boss</u>

Some people will do anything to get a raise or promotion including saying derogatory or negative things about a fellow employee. Most of the time the comments are false but to help further their career they will say or do anything. I have no idea how these individuals can face themselves in the mirror. It's sad but this is common practice in the corporate world. I think this type of behavior is sickening and totally reprehensible.

➤ <u>Going To The Doctor For Every Little Ache And Pain</u>

Every time this friend of mine caught a cold, or had a new ache or pain, she went to the doctor. Is her behavior right? No—first of all there are no cures for the common cold and why waste your time for every little ache? I'm sure you can find more useful things to occupy your time. On the other hand, I went 20 years without going to a doctor. Now, is my behavior right? No, when you're 40+ you should go at least once a year for a physical.

➤ <u>Children Using Backpacks With Wheels When They Don't Need Them</u>

What's this world coming to? No wonder there are so many children that are overweight and out of shape. Wheeled backpacks were created for those years when the load of books may be too much for a child who would be walking a good distance. Some young children were developing back problems because the weight of their books was too much for them and this was a solution. But in most cases they are not being used for these circumstances. Use common sense here. You might ask yourself what difference does it make whether or not a child carries their books? Children need all the exercise they can get. Even worse are those parents and grandparents who carry their backpacks for them. It also sets a bad precedent for years to come. As these kids get older they will continue to be lazy.

➢ <u>Having An Ego</u>

"Don't let your ego get too close to your position, so that if your position gets shot down, your ego doesn't go with it."
Colin Powell

Once you have acquired discipline the accomplishments have been piling up, there's a high probability that you start to get cocky. I'll make it simple – don't go there. With discipline you have an edge over so many people but learn to use it in a favorable manner - never let it get to your head.

BIBLIOGRAPHY

CBS News/60 Minutes II Internet Website. (2002, March 20). [Online]. Master Motivator. Available: http://www.cbsnews.com

Keen, Cathy. (1999, June 1). University of Florida Internet Website. Source: McAdaragh, Raymon. (1999, June 1). UF Study: Graveyard Shift May Have Benefits for Shift Workers. p. 1-2. [On-Line]. Available: http:www.napa.ufl.edu/99news/shift.htm

Kripke, Daniel. (2002, February 14). Archives of General Psychiatry. Sleep Less, Live Longer?

Perry, Ann. (2002, January 20). Personal Finance. Don't Give Your Kids Too Much, Experts Say. San Diego Union-Tribune. p. H1, H6

Roberts, Ozzie. (2002, March 29). Making It. Duo's Secret to Staying Young is Easy as A-B-C. San Diego Union-Tribune. p. E1, E11

Vos Savant, Marilyn. (2002, March 3). Ask Marilyn. Parade Magazine. p. 21

About the Authors

Karen Willi

Karen Willi spent 6 years climbing the computer industry ladder from 1984-1990. She then became a military spouse and her career shifted to government contract as well as a myriad of Civil Service jobs for the next 7 years. A few of those positions included data analyst work for the Army, Naval Telecommunications messaging to ships and Air Force medical administration providing critical data for pre-deployed squadrons. In 1997 she settled into her full-time CEO position of the Willi Family Corporation (WFC) to be a stay at home Mom. WFC is a fast-paced, highly mobile operation, which serves its customers throughout their entire lifecycle. She is now an editor, co-author and website advisor for Harris Kern's Enterprise Computing Institute.

Harris Kern

A world-renowned author, publisher, lecturer, and IT consultant, Harris Kern is the industry's leading mind on simplifying IT – and making it work. His extensive IT background serves as the foundation for his best-selling books. As executive editor of *Harris Kern's Enterprise Computing Institute*, he united the industry's leading minds to publish "how-to" textbooks on critical IT issues. The series includes titles such as: "Managing IT as an Investment", "Building Professional Services", "IT Services", "IT Organization", "IT Systems Management", "Technology Strategies", "High Availability", "IT Automation" and "Software Development". Harris also authored the *New Enterprise* series featuring: "Building the New Enterprise," and "Discipline: Six Steps to Unleashing Your Hidden Potential", an autobiography revealing successful management of both personal and professional life.

4213954

Made in the USA
Lexington, KY
04 January 2010